THE ELOQUENT POEM

THE
ELOQUENT POEM

128 CONTEMPORARY POEMS
AND THEIR MAKING

Edited by Elise Paschen

A Karen & Michael Braziller Book

PERSEA BOOKS / NEW YORK

Compilation and introduction copyright © 2019 by Elise Paschen

Because this page cannot accommodate all copyright credits,
pages 281–284 shall constitute an extension of the copyright page.

Persea Books, Inc.
90 Broad Street
New York, NY 10004

Library of Congress Cataloging-in-Publication Data

Names: Paschen, Elise, editor.
Title: The eloquent poem : 128 contemporary poems and their making /
edited by Elise Paschen.
Description: New York : Persea Books, [2019] | "A Karen & Michael Braziller book." |
Includes index.
Identifiers: LCCN 2018049836 | ISBN 9780892555000 (original trade pbk. : alk. paper)
Subjects: LCSH: American poetry.
Classification: LCC PS584.E48 2019 | DDC 811.008—dc23
LC record available at https://lccn.loc.gov/2018049836

Book design and composition by Rita Lascaro
Typeset in Garamond Premier Pro
Manufactured in the United States of America
Printed on acid-free paper

CONTENTS

COLLAGE POEMS

INTRODUCTION

At the heart of *The Eloquent Poem* beats the teachings of my college professor, Seamus Heaney, the great Irish poet and Nobel Laureate. I studied with Seamus when I was an undergraduate at Harvard University and participated in several of his classes, including one of the first poetry workshops he taught there. Each week Seamus would guide us through close readings of poems by the great masters. He brought in, for example, Elizabeth Bishop's "The Art of Losing," Dante Alighieri's Canto 5 from the *Inferno,* and drafts of William Butler Yeats's "Coole Park 1929." I still vividly remember his writing prompts (he called them "notions"), based on such poems, an ars poetica; an aubade; an echo poem; a villanelle, a litany. He talked about dramatizing the self into myth or into another character. He questioned: "How do you escape out of your experience into something greater, beyond it?" These suggestions reverberated with me and, as I began teaching my own poetry workshops, I would dedicate each class according to a different mode of writing.

The Eloquent Poem is designed with these various modes in mind. It is divided into sections by poetic approach—some formal, some occasional, and some thematic. What's more, this book includes original, never-before-published poems (many written specifically for it) by some of our best poets—many eminent (Billy Collins, Cornelius Eady, Martín Espada, Joy Harjo, Marilyn Nelson, and Eleanor Wilner, for example), some just emerging—representing diverse cultural and aesthetic backgrounds: a multiplicity of voices and a variety of styles and approaches to writing poems.

The zeitgeist of this anthology offered some intriguing overlaps. For the Ekphrastic section, both Lloyd Schwartz and David Yezzi submitted poems about the same painting by Titian, "The Flaying of Marsyas." Meanwhile, the painter Richard Diebenkorn influenced Tess Taylor's ekphrastic, "Notes on a Diebenkorn," and Alexandra Teague's mirror poem, "Studio with Blackened Windows." Kimiko Hahn's collage poem, "Things I Am Beginning to Forget," and Rigoberto González's list poem, "Things I Find in Abuela's Bathroom Closet," both owe debts to Sei Shonagon's *The Pillow Book.* In the Myth section, Grace Schulman, Edward Hirsch and Richard Tillinghast approached the story of Genesis from three differing perspectives. The late poet Agha Shahid Ali (my own beloved friend) influenced several works in the Poems in Form section, including William Wadsworth's "World Gone Wrong" and Tina Chang's

"Vivid Isolation: A Ghazal." That Poems in Form section offers examples of multiple traditional forms—from haiku to sestina. Although we received many poems purporting to be sonnets, I kept waiting for the right ones to serve as the models for *all* sonnets. Rosanna Warren sent us her roguish poem, "The Crux," and Jordi Alonso submitted a how-to-write-a-sonnet sonnet, whose more straightforward rhyme scheme and rhythm counter the slant rhymes and lineation of Warren's poem.

I have always been intrigued with the writing process, so I asked the contributors to write about the genesis of their included poems and to talk about how each one fits into its specific chapter. You will find fascinating and moving statements by the contributors about the makings of their poems at the end of this book. Each commentary is its own mini lesson about writing.

Throughout my life, I have assumed many different roles in the poetry community—from a young student poet to published author to editor to arts administrator and professor—and, of course, reader! All of these perspectives have given me a view of the multilayered world of writing. My hope is this anthology will allow you to shake up your own relationship to poetry. While conceived of for a semester-long course, and arranged to be suitable for one, *The Eloquent Poem* is a treasury for anyone who wants to explore all that contemporary American poetry has to offer.

Elise Paschen

THE ELOQUENT POEM

ARS POETICA

The term *ars poetica* comes from the Latin ("the art of poetry") and may be defined as a poem about the act of writing a poem. How do you describe the mystery, the evanescence of creating a poem? How do you suggest the intangible on the page? In a certain sense, almost any poem could be seen as an ars poetica, as each poem reflects its own nature. However, when you deliberately decide to write an ars poetica, you attempt to offer a glimpse of your own personal aesthetic or relationship to poetry itself.

In Seamus Heaney's celebrated ars poetica, "Digging," he compares his father's labor of digging for potatoes with his own art of inscribing words with the pen, concluding "But I've no spade to follow men like them. // Between my finger and my thumb / The squat pen rests. / I'll dig with it.

So, in writing an ars poetica you tap into your own creative process and create a metaphor of language for that vision or impulse.

JOY HARJO

Break My Heart

There are always flowers,
Love cries, or blood.

Someone is always leaving
By death, truck, or heartbreak.

The heart is a fist.
It pockets prayer or holds rage.

It's a timekeeper.
Music maker, or backstreet truth teller.

Baby, baby, baby
You can't say what's been said

Before, though even words
Are creatures of habit.

You cannot force poetry
With a ruler, at a desk.

Mystery is blind, but wills you
To untie the cloth, in eternity.

The police with their guns
Cannot enter here to move us off our lands
Or kill our babies.

Someone will lift from the earth
Without wings.

Another will fall from the sky
Through the knots of a tree.

Chaos is primordial.
All words have roots here.

History will always find you, and wrap you
In its thousand arms.

You will never sleep again
Though you will never stop dreaming.

The end can only follow the beginning.
And it will zigzag through time, governments, and lovers.

Be who you are, even if it kills you.

It will. Over and over again.
Even as you live.

Break my heart, why don't you?

Martha Rhodes

Delivery

A long arm dipped in to rescue right where
I fell off the boat. Too late, late, late for I
have drifted already far. Shivering, and the sea darkens.
A ladder, a rope, that persistent arm—
It is a wave drives me home.

ELEANOR WILNER

The Uses of What Is Hollow

Was it hungry innocence for good
that filled things out: the monuments we visited
as children, Lincoln in his high stone seat,
Monticello settled on its hill, its owner still revered:
how fine to dream the pastoral, without those leering
peasants that Breughel caught in oil and fixative:
dim eyes, mouths gaping, wet with pleasure
at the painful execution of a god—the lynch mobs
of history, whose shadow marks the hollow,
the emblem of the tree itself disgraced.

el condor pasa . . . can you hear that haunting sound, uncanny
in its beauty, panpipes of Peru, that mime the sound of wind,
the spread of wings, the soaring beauty of the condor high
above the Andes, glory in the pass—*and, when Pan*
thought he had captured her, he held instead
only the tall marsh reeds . . . and made of hollow loss
a song, and of the vulture's circle overhead, such music
that every reed could sing when given breath,
pure melody born of wind and emptiness,
so piercing and so high, *el condor pasa* overhead . . .
look up: no, higher! do you see him now? His wings outspread,
the V that children draw when they mean *bird* and *far*
and *sky*, the condor gives the emptiness its size,
in search of death on which it feeds, and as it flies, the pan-
pipes play, the music is so lovely, it could stop the breath.

Mai Der Vang

Ars Poetica

As in a glitch that wishes to idle in my abdomen,
            flicking ever onward.

As in a botched chronology of desire, fire-fully
            and powdered in the season of my name.

As in olfactory seductions: juniper after rain, iron
            after gale, rosemary under snow.

Landings of the elder lore must have had a quill
            to its skin but that is not how my voyager arrives.

I am recklessly prehistoric, fumbling and haphazard
            underneath the ultraviolet.

I am surrendering to the pinky of my childhood as it misfires
            out of a sycamore from the eighties.

What's left to hear isn't the lunar announcement or a light-washed
            dew or the hollow dud that shatters into glass.

            Just the antique of a birth swallowing
                        open my sternum

ALAN MICHAEL PARKER

The Lights Burn Blue

Outside, a bluebird and an indigo bunting
take turns at the feeder, confusing me,
which one is blue. I blame the sky,

I do, every time I try
to marry the sky to a particular blue,
it's gone, and then me too.

When I was a boy poet
in a canoe, and the blue moon
was oh-so in the river,

and the river was oh-so to the sea,
my open mouth went O to every Ooh.
I made the blue woohoo.

But now, because of the birds,
and my body inside
the room built of my feelings,

I know the poems I made were wrong.
Because blue is a unit of time.
Because each blue measures

how long is blue,
flashing outside my window,
pretending to be a bird.

ALLISON SEAY

Mother (of Poetry)

A person, for example, can lie in her bed all afternoon—
or all her life—and never know

where the true center is.

It's summer again. High sky in the persimmon tree.
Laundry baking on the line and a bullfrog in the late morning

among the tall grasses. There is no certainty
except for beauty.

Not in the world, not in the body:

I cannot know precisely nor intimately the very things
holding me together: not the center

of the small of my own back,
not the nape of my own neck, not the soul.

But evidence of the finite is also evidence of the infinite.
One is born of the other

and there is no such thing as nothing.

KIMBERLY JOHNSON

The Invention of the F-hole

Run your thumb under the trembling
       String along
    The fretted neck, and back

The curve and burnish of the sounding board
       Then rim a fingertip
    Over and into the cutout lip,

Luthier, to the spruce's smooth expose.
       What the knife knows
    Is its own sweet progress

Through the woodgrain. What the woodgrain knows
       Will at last hum
    Through what passage the blade opens,

Released like a long sigh into the world's
       Unwitting ear.
    The whimsied engineer

Who first this flourish scribed aspired less
       To the nice math
    Of resonant frequencies

And pressure differentials than to the curl
       Shaving pale
    And warm into his palm,

The woman whose whorls he longed to touch.
       What other love
    Can explain the plaintive

Timbre of this Cremonese fancy?:
       Unanswerable
    Strain through the finial's swell

To the hearing's inmost chamber. His tender
        Error of exchange
     To us as a heritage remains;

Belated even to our own fleet loves,
        We invent
     For every one an accident

To be tooled as a seal into anything
        We can hold.
     Thus, luthier, do you bring

Your knives to bed. Thus do you wear my ring.

CORNELIUS EADY

Ars Poetica

Sometimes I feel
My relationship to American Poetry
Is a lot like the Halloween
I stood at the door of one of my aunts,
The sister of my mother, the one
Who lived in a small trimmed house
Married without children. There I was,
Not having much to do with her life,
Though she lived right across the street.

In the arch of her door,
Paper bag open, without a mask,
I think I wanted recognition, the fame
Of being the son of her sister. But
She turned, and who was I,
Walking un-kissed
To the next house, who am I now?

LITANIES, CATALOGS, & LISTS

The organizing principle in litany poems is *anaphora* (from the Greek: "a carrying up or back"), the repetition of a word or phrase at the beginning of a sentence. The accumulation of these repetitions creates a spell-like effect upon the poem. By using repetition at the beginning of the sentence, you forecast something which is expected yet also expansive, allowing the lines to open up or unfurl. A classic example of this repetition is used by N. Scott Momaday in "The Delight Song of Tsoai-Talee," which begins : "I am a feather on the bright sky / I am the blue horse that runs in the plain / I am the fish that rolls, shining, in the water. . . . " Oral poetry relied heavily on this use of repetition, offering poets, such as Homer, mnemonic devices to remember the lines of the poem recited.

The catalog poem or list poem is another playful form which allows poets to accumulate a miscellany of objects and counter them against each other. Some of the subjects of the list poems in this section include titles on a bookshelf, names of American poets, and the objects a child discovers in a grandmother's bathroom. Through the accumulation of minutiae, a universe unfolds.

ANGELA JACKSON

For Our People

(Homage to Margaret Walker's "For My People.")

for our people everywhere singing
their gospels and their rap, their blues,
R&B, and their jazz, their soul and their neo soul, all Great Black Music,
scuffling, scrimping, struggling to get by,
for our people working as wage slaves,
in collars blue, white and pink, doing the best
they can with what they have, hoping
it will not be taken away with a pink slip,
a sudden slip from a parapet, on cement
into disability or welfare, or not,
hustling to keep from being crushed,
on the unemployment line.

for our people
for the way of years sipping summer from a tall glass of ice water,
buttermilk and cornbread out of a mayonnaise jar,
years testing watermelon, cutting a plug of sweetness,
knocking on the round or oblong to listen to the taste,
for the excellence of young boys running like they stole something,
but only owning themselves and the strength in their legs
and girls who could keep up before breasts held them back.

for our people and red kool-aid days,
for smothered chicken and our cries smothered
in a world that did not adore us, but ignored us
or worse and ran us back on the other side of the viaduct
where we belonged, not in the wild world we could conquer
or excel in, given the gates opening and tools for redress.

for our people everywhere
growing gardens on vacant lots, training roses
and black eyed susans and perennials in front yards, raking
leaves and shoveling snow, scooping doo, and picking up
litter, washing and ironing out the wrinkles of everyday existence

for our people
running and hiding with nowhere to go, watching
television and movies looking for ourselves, searching
books and the nooks and crannies of history
for a glimpse of what was waylaid, and what is to be,
in barbershops and beauty parlors and ice cream parlors
and the stone faces in funeral parlors, picking up children
from school from daycare, taking them to football, soccer,
baseball, tennis, basketball, volleyball, having a ball
at family reunions, on Saturday nights

for our people who came in chains,
tortured over turbulent waters, broken
hearted, and broken tongued, and broken magic,
broken bloodlines, strangled and whipped, distraught
and driven to the edge of the mind, and beyond
for our people leaping to the sea, feeding sharks and myths and cautionary
tales, surviving the journey to reach auction blocks,
a prurient pedestal for deposed queens, and chieftains, villagers
humiliated, abused, raped, and riddled with misery into
exquisite survivals, changing vocabulary and clothes, changing
into sleek panthers and superheroes, making the world safe
for demonstrations of protest and affection, all beauty and love,
scapegoated, pilloried, denied the excellence we bring

for our people grasping for gadgets and genuflecting
to electric celebrity, worshipping trinkets and noisome
symbols that blink and itch the eyes, gaming and gambling
and laughing to keep from crying, and crying laughing,
cracking up, and falling out, drinking suicide, and spilling milk
and blood, gunned down under lampposts, in playgrounds,
bloodied in drive-bys, in alleys, in living rooms, in bed sleeping

for our people bludgeoned by police and each other,
killed by presumptuous watchers, taxed for Black and driving while Black,
shot in the back, falsely convicted, sentenced to dwell alone, and

want to be redeemed, incarcerated in stone, tracked in department stores,
harassed, stalked in malls, and all the places people spent and sell,
our people selling loose squares, oils, socks and peanuts
on the corners of our desperate longing, for hair, for nails, for body
graffiti

for our people in the casinos, scheming in pennies from heaven
with one armed pirates, dreaming in die and cards and dealers,
dreaming numbers and playing them til they hit,
for our people drowning in spirits, burning throats and pockets
losing it all, spoiling livers, lungs, and kidneys, hearts with too much,
each of us addicted to drugs of fashion, to ancient hurt,
choosing crabs in a barrel or lifting as we climb, each one teach one.

for our people who do not belong to me but to all of us for we belong
to each other, must hold each other in heart and mind
for our people in the citadels of learning and the one room school house,
in the storefronts of funeral parlor fans and the cathedrals of painted windows
and arched ceilings that lend toward sky
for our people in the baptismal pool, in white robes on the edge of the river,
for our people, chanting and praying and hoping for a sweeter brew to sip
and savor

let a new earth arise
let justice pour like trembling rain and mercy prevail as plentiful fields.
let our strength be matched by vulnerable honesty of heart
may resilience be our guide, for we will stumble and then will rise
more able having fallen, more beautiful having met each other
along the way as we lifted each other up, hero-people who go out of their way
for love, and stay on the way of goodness

let our people be the people who remember and believe that love is all our
                                                                    portions
all our currencies and all are one, each of us injured or exalted, betrayer or
                                                            betrayed, muted

and declamatory, all one, each of us all of us, each a private star beloved in the
universe,
each of us creature of burdens and singing angel merged as one, alive and
moving upward
holding on and lifting this earth, our house, precious and precarious, and God
be our witness
between this gravity and this grace. hold tight and fly.

Joy Ladin

Political Poem

I remember the whiteness of my mother's love,
the coupon-clipping whiteness

of her lower-middle-class love,
the brown round injustice

of the pennies she clutched
in the white-knuckled fingers

of her love.
The whiteness of her childhood Depression

and the whiteness of mine
shone like lights in a closet

we dared not open. No one could look
at the motions we went through

and say they saw anything
but whiteness and love.

Whiteness was a privilege I exercised by playing
with the individually wrapped slices

of her love. Whiteness
was strewn all around us, the bric-a-brac of whiteness

crammed the basement and attic
of the white house

on the all-white street
of our all-white neighborhood.

Whiteness was our home.
It kept us under surveillance

even when we were alone.
Eyes disguised as carpet stains

watched my mother and I rehearse
the whiteness that was to me

invisible as love.
I was a child playing a child.

She was a mother battering batter,
filling buttered cupcake tins

with vanilla, butter, egg, sugar, water and flour,
all the ingredients of whiteness we mixed

into the whiteness of love.

ANNA LEAHY

From the Word *Go*

Go wild, go dry, go get her, get up and go. Go into effect and out of fashion. Go over big and over someone's head. Go straight; go stag. Have a go at the roof; go through something, anything. Go steady; go overboard. Go the distance through the motions. Go for broke and into detail. Go in one ear and on and on, scot free, from bad to worse.

Quraysh Ali Lansana

descendent

i am holding my brothas hand
he walks ahead of me centuries

resist sixteen nineteen coffles
& whips in a sick society

resist eighteen thirty-three crackers
& furious dogs in a sick society

resist nineteen twenty-one noose
& mob in a sick society

resist nineteen fifty-five judge
& crow in a sick society

resist nineteen sixty-eight law
& order in a sick society

resist nineteen years of burge
& socket in a sick society

resist two-thousand thirteen cages
& apathy in a sick society

i am holding my sistas hand
she walks centuries ahead of me

Aliki Barnstone

Waiting for Greece's Fate on Serifos

1   All night long the wind banged one of the balcony doors against the wall.

2   A woman is drowning and I pound her chest until she throws up salt water and breathes. All the while, I can hardly hear words; the wind is boxing my ears.

3   Bad dreams, heartburn—I could not rouse myself to secure the door with a rock. Maybe that's a metaphor for rulers. They're too tired to wake from the nightmare and move the rock, too deeply held by the dream.

4   I put the laundry in the washer. We take hot showers, wash dishes with water flowing from the tap. When I water the garden, the water flows down our street toward the sea or into the manhole near our house. When I was younger, no water flowed from the tap for weeks at a time, except in the wee hours of night. We hauled water from the fountain in the square. We left the dry taps open at night, so the sputter and gush would wake us and we'd fill our buckets.

5   My friend writes that if Greece goes back to the drachma, it will take generations for the nation to recover, if ever.

6   There is still a lion-head fountain on the footpath from the village to the port.

7   I run cool water over my wrists, splash water on my face, drink from my cupped hands.

8   A truck rolls off the ferry, loudspeakers blasting. We wait for the sound to come closer, to hear if he's selling melons, cherries, peaches, apricots, tomatoes, cucumbers or tables, chairs, sheets, and baskets or political propaganda.

9   People talk on their mobiles on the beach or scroll through their emails, texts, social media, and the news, the goddamn news. A woman sits on a folding chair, wrapped in a red towel, her hair still wet, her MacBook Air on her lap.

10   The banks are closed, except for the €60 a day Greeks are allowed to withdraw from ATMs. Pensioners who don't have debit cards line up at the back on the announced day, but the banks have no cash. The elderly are told to come back tomorrow or the next business day or the next.

11   Eric brings the map of the island that he bought when he visited 20 years ago. The map doesn't show the paved roads we drive every day, doesn't show the reservoir and the dam, doesn't show we have abundant water now and how much overflows into the sewers or into the sea.

Friday, July 3, 2015

BILLY COLLINS

The Afterlife of American Poets

Robert Frost sits on a log of gold.

T.S. Eliot, wearing a black suit, is looking at a peach.

Elizabeth Bishop has been transformed into a lighthouse.

William Carlos Williams moves through the atmosphere in a nimbus of white chickens.

John Berryman's beard is longer now, suspended in ether.

Frank O'Hara is running late for his lunch with God.

Ezra Pound rides around on a big radio, holding a blue pencil aloft.

Charles Olsen remains in his coffin trying to finish a talk he began in 1965.

Marianne Moore is escorted everywhere by a phalanx of Brooklyn Dodgers.

Wallace Stevens has created a new dominion composed of nothingness and blackbirds.

W. D. Snodgrass continues to walk through the universe, only now barefoot.

Walt Whitman is holding God in one hand and the devil in the other.

Jack Spicer is inside a green beer bottle in the middle of a limitless city park.

W. H. Auden, still encased in flesh, pads around in atomic slippers.

Allen Ginsberg, wearing only red underwear, is looking for someone among the clouds.

William Stafford is at a desk surrounded by deer and headlights.

Weldon Kees is bobbing to the surface of paradise.

Emily Dickinson—the light has stopped on her face and dress.

CHRISTINA PUGH

Litany

How can I learn the language of a landscape?
The spume is relentless, beneath its cape of trees.
The spume is concentric around the rock-island.
The trees are foresting, leaning from the shore.
I can see the leaf-cover hover at the water.
The olive and agave are reaching for no one.

What shall I rub on my skin to make it permeable?
How to burn a path from the sea to my interior?
How do I say to my cell walls, *Receive?*
Which tires first, the eyes or the memory?

Impregnable means that you can be with child,
or never. A fortified wall might be
impregnated, or never. *O wall!* lamented
Pyramus, played by a mechanical. A word
like that has caught a paradox within it.

My outer or inner wall is impermeable:
the fulcrum over which I'll drape
the concept of the body. How porous
is the alabaster shaped into angels

studding the garden near the ruinous sea!
At night, could I constellate and slip
along the universe? How to still the flowering
that integrates our bodies' walls? The sea
is relentless—an army, and bright.
What will I scatter in the garden of the sea?

Select an Answer

A. Inside the spiral of the canal, a shining table where the patient cannot be touched. A boy hums at a window and hears the hum murmur back at him as the glass rattles the way a dragonfly's cellophane wings shatter themselves in flight.

B. The window overlooks an audience.

C. The audience swigs its narcotics and looks down into the theater where a body lay open like a piazza and the terrible light opens it further onto the stage where a language arranges and arranges, only able to keep the darkness still for awhile.

D. The verb of the saw. The verb of the hand.

KIMIKO HAHN

Titles from Harold's Shelf, A Portrait

The Secret Life of Puppets

The Criminal Prosecution and Capital Punishment of Animals

The Art of Harvey Kurtzman

The Faith Instinct

Nameless Indignities

The Science of Evil

All-True Crime

The Body in Parts

Chain Saw Confidential

From the Annals of Crime and Rascality

Leave it to the Ladies

Murder at Smutty Nose

Celia Thaxter Selected Poems

Jay's Journal of Anomalies

Hunger: an unnatural history

ELIZABETH SPIRES

Questions for Google

What does it mean and why does it matter?
How do I get from here to there?
Where is the line that cannot be crossed?
Why is the first time the best?

Who will be coming and when will they get here?
How long will it last before it is over?
Who has the right and why do they have it?
Who is the most important one?

What did it mean and why did it matter?
If all is lost, how will I find it?
If not now, then when?
Are you *real*? Do you even exist?

Rigoberto González

Things I Find in Abuela's Bathroom Closet

A green towel
A blue towel
Both towels with loose threads like spaghetti strings
I cut them off once but the next week they had grown out like weeds
Abuela darns Abuelo's socks and says, Just let them be
A white towel with a hotel logo
It's the nicest towel she has, though she doesn't remember who
        stayed at that hotel, or who brought it home
A purple washcloth, its corners stained black
Shoe polish, though Abuelo doesn't have shoes that need polishing
The polish smells of gloved gentlemen in black and white movies,
        their shoes as shiny as their top hats, do they polish the hats as well?
Abuela says, Their mustaches too
How they dance like long pencils on the ballroom floor
A box of batteries, big candle-thick batteries. For flashlights, I supposed
A wig
A very strange wig, like a dead crow on the road
I put it on and it itches when I spin it on my head
Abuela says, Don't play with that
And I say, Please, at least until Abuelo gets home
And Abuela says, Don't you dare tell anyone
I grab Abuela's flowered bathrobe and pretend to walk past
        those gentlemen in their shiny hats, how I blush when they
        tip them and whisper pretty things that sound French like *amour!*
My wig comes alive like a cat and purrs
Abuela says, Silly boy
A box of bobby pins
A box of incense
A box of matches
A box of soap, the lavender I breathe when I press my face against Abuela
A tube of red lipstick, though I have never seen Abuela wear make-up,
        her brown lips so sun-chapped from working in the fields since the 60s
A blue tin of moisturizer
A red tin of cream that smells like rancid mayo
Abuela says, Don't touch that, it burns
And burn it did, my fingers catch fire and I scream

Abuela shakes her head as she washes my hands
She wipes them clean with the green towel
I glare at the tin that reads Belly Jelly Burner Cream
Abuela says, I don't know who left it there
She goes back to her needle and thread
I go back to the closet
A black bra like two funny hats sewn together
A black bra like a split open coconut
I'm about to ask Abuela when we Abuelo's truck pulls up
Abuela says, Put everything away
I shove the boxes in
I push the towels in
I hide the wig and the polish
But when I stick my arm inside the cubbyhole I feel another box
A box I missed the first time
A box deep inside the closet's belly
A plastic penis
A plastic penis like a flashlight
A plastic penis with the big fat batteries
A plastic penis with knob I can turn
A plastic penis that buzzes but won't light up
I hold it to my chest and it hums to me
It's what those ladies in the black and white movies must feel
        when their gentlemen press their dark mustaches
        against their lady hearts—bird courting another bird

EPISTLES & POSTCARDS

An epistle is a letter poem that can be addressed to anyone or anything. In writing an epistle, you build a personal bridge to someone living, someone departed, or from the past, or maybe even fictitious. The epistle simulates the form of the letter and offers an invitation to a correspondence; some epistles include a reply from the original recipient.

While reading an epistle, we have that sense of encountering a private exchange between the letter writer and its recipient. There is an intimacy, even a thrill, in this sense of reading a communication between two, as we are not the intended reader.

What does it mean to write something to someone else knowing a third party will read it—or that if they do, so will others? The reader does not necessarily know the history that exists between these two people, and successful epistles resist overexplaining, instead creating a balance between what's personal and what's declared. Ideally, a reader understands the ethos of the relationship, even without knowing all its details.

Meanwhile, the postcard poem sends a quick missive about a place in time. Its beauty is in creating a snapshot, a shorthand, an encapsulation in a compact space.

Ira Sukrungruang

Our Fault Is We Love Too Much

Dear Lorna—Today you came to me
in wind with a hint of loneliness. I hope
I am wrong. I hope you are well and finding yourself.
Let me tell you about the alligator
I saw this afternoon. It was in the river, head and back
poking out like a mountain range,
and for long minutes we stared
at each other. There are signs
all over the park. *Beware.* Last month it devoured
a pug. But today, it remained a log at the edge.
Some days we are vicious. Some days we are still.
Today I am melancholic, which makes me easy
prey. There is nothing more vulnerable
than a person in thought, and my thought is this:
the heart is the easiest muscle
to bruise and the hardest one to heal. The sky is so blue
I think I might drown. I'm happy. I'm not saying
this to convince myself. I'm saying this
because happiness is possible despite our scars. Or maybe,
because of them. An osprey digs its claws
into a fish on top of a light pole. What's weak
feeds. I promise to be in better contact. I hope
you are in a good place. Ira.

ELIZABETH MACKLIN

With Love from Ainezalandia

The size of the market in Ainezalandia,
the municipal market down by the speaking river,
is the size of a ferryboat: yellow as any crossing
to Staten Island—spruce-trimmed goldenrod,
steaming upriver on the speaking ebb tide
but stationary, spoken for here right now by seagulls,
come for the 1 P.M. close,
speaking out—wheeling—for scraps
from the fish floor.

          Coming even on Sundays and Mondays,
when the fish floor's closed, to wheel and squall.
They helped me to know their desires—
aineza, ainendi—or my desires,
ainendi, aineza. Or our desires.
Perhaps for dailiness above all.

Cynthia Atkins

Dear Art

Flash point: I was put to bed last night
with your railroad kiss. I awoke with a ladder
in my mouth, tropes of people climbing out
in a death choke. Your tawdry laundry-line
of images blowing manic through needling wind.
I was always in earshot, but you were first to leave
the party. A hard lullaby, I feared you were
a household word in a ghost town.
My silence was torrential, a bombshell.
A swamp of worms rilling into words—
into cordial song. In debt and spent,
yours truly, truly yours.

MOLLY McCULLY BROWN AND SUSANNAH NEVISON

from *In the Field Between Us*

Dear M—
For once I'm glad to be led
to water and asked to drink, to be
untracked, unfollowed,
to let the light in our mouths beat
against every rough surface, until
we know every given thing by its white
marrow, until the only world we know
is a raised root system, a garden
of twined scars that threads our skin
like the river we can't outrun. M,
let's set them loose from their cages, the birds,
set the songs loose from their throats,
and crack open our own to welcome
what may come: another way to speak,
a little song, an elegy for all the selves
we couldn't save, or wouldn't.

Dear S—
If our throats crack open
as we reach the bank
and they're the last whole
parts of us to yield a river
when we're butterflied,
if what pours out
is everything we've carried
on the current all our lives:
stones and steel, scraps
of fabricated sky, the silt from
every drug that didn't dissolve
then *become* us. If it
comes loose and rushes
for the door we've shaped
and leaves us with an open
room to do our claiming in,
S, will we even recognize
the sounds we make, know
that their echoing means
grief or *knife* or *sister,*
want, arrival, or our names?

Dear M—
For want of arrival, a clear
syllable that opens across
the room or the field
between us, give me
instead the earth and silt
our names become
with each labored
step, the dust of our
names inconvenient and
undeniable in the light,
the way they collect in the corner
of a stranger's room, all
the ways they're uttered,
the ways we heed: give me
crooked bird, wildflower, chokeweed.
        Give me a picture of two girls
crouched low, a list of things
belonging to them: what
grows along the ground.
What turns back on itself
as it goes.

Dear S—
Chokeweed: small white flowers like bells
that crawl over all the canyons
and trees, every bed the girls
once occupied, all the bent bodies
bent again until they'd cease
hunting themselves, cease curling in.
Until they'd heed. S, let's make more
of it, let's spur it on, let's water it until
the girls sit down in the dust,
until it climbs their folded legs and up
then down their throats, until we cannot tell
them from the ground, from hills, muscle
from flower, from ringing, tell whatever
belonged to them from the field, tell
the field from wherever we are now.

TODD FULLER

Postcards to Etheridge Knight

1st Postcard:

Dear Teacher: I am
full of echoes tonight
as I curl into what's
left (~~in my memory~~) of
your voice:

"We free singers be,"
you proclaim (from
your moonlit headstone)
in Indiana. Indeed, we

free singers be/long
to streets and earth
and cosmic sub-
committees. We be/

come rejoicers of
Cupid's crimson
wings and willing
victims of his heinous
arrows.

2nd Postcard:

Dear Teacher: Our
free singing voices
be/seech orphans &
convicts & protesters

to raise the echoes
of their thoughts / to
locate the crosshairs
of their passions

and create a song for
the hungry, for factory
whistles (and the 500
whistling workers),
and their mothers

who wring their
hands with memories
of sunshine & gospel.

3rd Postcard:

Dearest Teacher: in
Oklahoma tonight
a full moon rises
against the profile
of our planet as

we drive by the
Etheridge Ranch
in Cushing. That's
when I remember
the cushion of y'r
graveled words.

My son says, "Who
is the moon?" And
my tongue cries
"Uncle Etheridge"
before I can shove
the words aside.

4th Postcard:

Dear Teacher: I am
poor tonight. And
I cannot send you
10 bucks for a pack
of Kools and a ½
case, as you
requested.

But someday, I'll
answer your letter,
which came too late.

Someday, I'll
give the breath of
these words to your
whiskers, which my
baby girl will grab
with both hands
& proclaim: *sing
free.*

ERIKA MEITNER

Letter to Hillary on the
Radical Hospitality of the Body

I want to tell you something about the body, though I'm not sure how to articulate it exactly. I've been trying all morning to write a meditation on the sensory, on touch, delineate between kinesthetic and haptic, and instead I am staring at the white hard-boiled egg I took from breakfast rolled on its side on my white desk. Instead, I am fielding texts from my sister who had a baby last week and says she has uncontrollable chills and wonders if this is normal hormonal post-partum stuff or what. I don't know the answer so I tell her to call her doctor in case it's an infection because it's Sunday and I'm at an artists' colony with period cramps and a slight hangover since last night a painter opened the massive barn where they keep sculptures-in-process, put some beer on ice, rigged up his phone, and threw a dance party where we did our best to lose ourselves in darkness and summer and Saturday night, Kendrick Lamar and Nicki Minaj, Kanye and even Aretha until our bodies stopped thinking of themselves at all and we were only movement—limbs pressing through air, helicopters, drummers, wind-up contraptions, turbine engines. Until we were all sweating profusely, taking turns standing in front of the lone fan, flapping our shirts up and out to let the generated wind cool skin we'd normally keep covered up. Outside the doors, split open to the rafters, there were fireflies pulsing mating codes, stars pushing forward their fused light, clouds trailing their dust across the face of the moon. Like them, we leave traces behind—of hair and skin, accumulations of bodily excess donated back to the earth. Like the ash I flick from the cigarette I smoke behind the barn, a measure of time and breath. Like spit and blood and cum and piss. I have let so many things and people enter and sometimes inhabit my body for lengths of time, they're uncountable, and I'm sure you have too despite the fact that the world tells us as women to stay vigilant and shut. This is not about void or gap or hole, what's missing or punched through or needs filling. Yesterday on the way here I passed two storefronts in the same strip mall—Big Boyz Guns & Ammo next to Serenity Counseling Center, and then near the Sheetz a hiker walking the shoulder of 460 carrying a giant wooden cross that was at least half the size of himself. This is where I'd insert something about violence and mindfulness, grace and perhaps suffering, but who knows why anyone carries anything around until it gets so heavy we set it down. Hillary, this isn't working; I don't know any more about the body than I did to begin with except that I was surprised I still remember how to dance with abandon—it had been years. We carry our movements, muscle memory, scars of all kinds inscribed on our skin, and inside us a space-time continuum that contains all the people and places we've touched and tasted and walked through and dwelled in, and as soon as we move through them they change and vanish so I will open myself again and again. What I'm trying to say in this small body of a poem is that our bodies themselves are without regrets—persistent and mortal and relentless.

CHRIS GREEN

After the Dragonflies

Dear Brother,
remember the day I said

I saw a dead body?
I count the lies.

You ran and ran, terrified,
up a hill. I followed

through the dead grass, until we
climbed out into dragonflies!—

hundreds shaped a whirlwind around
you, an embrace and a warning.

This habit of memory.
I refused to love you once. You,

my principal witness. Our otherness
mirrored in those insects who see

everywhere at once. One feels confined
sifting old summers for clues.

I cannot know you. It is the normal way.
The concentrics of growing up. Death

itself has been building, and forgetfulness.
I have been rearranging.

Lately, I've been opening deep drawers.
Things have come to that.

DONNA MASINI

Postcard: Morning Window, Venice

Though it looks like a dusty flat screen TV
I want you to see the way this Venetian sky
effaces the famous 150 canals, and fades
into morning. Yesterday I left St. Mark's to shop,
escape the anxious mosaic epitaphs, the crazed saints
climbing the walls. There's always tomorrow.
I'd love to walk with you tomorrow, but I'll be hunting,
an old man said last week. The kind of random anecdote
I save for you. Were you not dead, you'd laugh.
Venice is still dying. Shiny. Nothing to buy.
I wish I were here.

POEMS IN FORM

This section offers a variety of forms to explore including: sonnets, a fourteener, a haiku, a sestina, a villanelle, a ballad, a triolet, a ghazal, quatrains, as well as excursions into meter. Some of the poems here experiment with rhyme and off-rhyme as well as repetitions in various disguises.

When you explore poems in form, you play with notions of constraint. In doing so, you might discover that, by learning a verse structure, and then breaking the rules, you will unearth a new articulation for your poetry. As Richard Wilbur observes about traditional forms, "they can liberate you from whatever narrow track your own mind is running on, and prompt it to be loose and inventive, to entertain possibilities it hadn't foreseen." Tinkering with different verse structures you may discover patterns and repetitions through sound and rhythm which you then can dislodge. Working with form allows you to pursue directions you had not intended, unleashing linguistic surprises.

Rosanna Warren

The Crux

Like playing dominoes on death row through the bars
        so the little black rectangles form a cross
        on the prison hallway floor
and the dots wink like stars

while the corridor drives in merciless fluorescence
        to a vanishing point the camera
        captures as a chunk of dark:
is this what it's like to finger the end of a sentence

that doesn't conclude? Let the dots hook up, hold off:
        we are convicted if not
        convinced: keep the game
going, the pattern may hide a proof

the crime wasn't what we thought.
An end will come. But in a different plot.

JORDI ALONSO

How To:

A fourteenth of a sonnet is now done
And five more feet will mean we've got a seventh.
In this third line we get to rhyme—it's fun.
And now we find ourselves a fourth to heaven.
The second quatrain starts another set
Of rhymes. Here's a substitution. See,
Straight iambs are as boring as they get.
A prosodist would call this end rhyme "D".
Here is a perfect spot to start a turn,
Or give more time to our argument:
Because this happened here's what I have learned
Not what I knew, but what the experience meant.
And finally, to sum up, joke, or hit
our sonnet home, we end this line with wit.

JEANETTA CALHOUN MISH

Reckoning

A convent of thirteen whiptail lizards on the back porch
females-all, who reproduce parthenogenically:
develops her embryos from unfertilized egg cells.
This rapt desire to be birthed from the head of Hecate.

Seven years after her burial, my mother appears
proffering an apology shrouded in satin rags.
A sapphire sky clotted with clouds pronounces you *guilty.*
Late night under shy new moon insinuates *maybe not.*

Condemnation is mere theory. Forgiveness is praxis.
Human memory is arranged by spatial metaphor—
in my memento cabinet: fist, belt, muted whimper.
This raw desire to learn to forget stygian spaces.

The body, they say, keeps score, a count exact and submerged.
In dusk woven of wind and shivering leaves, no quarter.

Hecate (HEK-a-tee): The goddess of magic, crossroads, moon, ghosts,
witchcraft and necromancy (the undead).

MOLLY PEACOCK

Haiku

A spider skitters
from the unfurled yoga mat.
It goes where it goes.

TONY TRIGILIO

The UFO Incident

*The following story is based on actual transcripts of the reel-to-reel tapes
made by Betty (Estelle Parsons) and Barney (James Earl Jones) under hypnosis
by Dr. Simon (Barnard Hughes, the veteran character actor who played
a nervous con man named Jack Spicer in a 1971 episode of the television series
Cannon—not that Jack Spicer, of course, the poet who claimed that writing
was the equivalent of dictated radio transmissions received from Martians).*

Autumn sunset, the White Mountains, sky rash-red like a photo of the Martian
horizon—so begins our captivity narrative. All the action will occur on tape,
recovered memories unspooling in Dr. Simon's office. For the teleplay writers,
the great challenge, it seems, was to make Betty and Barney Hill's hypnotherapy
sessions terrifying to viewers accustomed to paint-by-number 1970s police series
procedurals. Studio execs were nervous about casting interracial actors to play

the Hills, but, all the same, green-lighted the aliens' blue skin. C-list actors play
blue astronauts the Hills claimed were gray. Our spacemen first appear marching
out of the dark New England wood with the creepy, anthropological seriousness
of zookeepers. After several cuts between close-ups of Dr. Simon's rolling tape
machine and these creatures sheathed in blue latex—I'd have to be hypnotized
to believe their body-stockings were actually skin—I decided I couldn't write

this poem without looking up who wore the alien suits. So where does a writer
go for sestina research? Wikipedia and IMDB, natch. The actor who played
"The Leader," Lou Wagner, first made a name for himself uttering the mesmerizing
words of the chimp Lucius—"You can't trust the older generation!"—in *Planet
of the Apes* (a precocious teen, he was Zira's nephew), before Taylor went traipsing
down the beach with his mute galpal, Nova, their horse performing a series

of alternating trots and gallops before stumbling upon that film's most serious
and arresting image: Lady Liberty, buried to her shoulders in the sand, written
off as an ancient, apocalyptic ruin. The Leader is the alien on Dr. Simon's tapes
Barney feared most. No longer the charming Lucius, now Wagner played
The Leader like the brute Nazi Barney felt he was—not some little green Martian.
These latexed, cat-eyed Zeta Reticulans were rapists. It took hypnotherapy

to reveal the Hills' repressed sexual trauma. That is, if you believe hypnosis
recovers actual memories (Simon was skeptical). What could be more serious
and alienating (whether the Hills actually were probed by Zeta Reticulans

or it was a fraud invented by a couple who should've been writing
sci-fi) than to have your assault dismissed by skeptics who claim you're playing
a hoax? Would the publicity-shy Hills fake an attack, then document it on tape

during hypnosis? Not that these questions actually emerge from the script
or any kind of serious cinematography. After all, this is a film that chose to play
aliens in fetish outfits and waste footage on countless close-ups of reel-to-reel tapes.

ALLISON JOSEPH

Villanelle of Margaritas

One part lime juice, three parts tequila,
and two parts Cointreau, a triple sec.
How passionately do margaritas

take me over, make me quiver,
quick of mouth and loose of neck.
One part lime juice, three parts tequila,

not a mix from a box, but silver—
called *blanco*—tequila. Don't wreck
how passionately a margarita

can taste with juice that won't deliver
flavor—always fresh-squeezed, no dreck.
One part lime juice, three parts tequila,

enough Cointreau so you shiver
as this mix goes down, the check
gets fat. Passionately, have more margaritas

with me, a few glasses, then a river,
let's close down this bar—what the heck!
One part lime juice, three parts tequila—
More passion, more you, more margaritas.

JUDITH BAUMEL

Ballad of the Bronx Zoo's Beloved

Lulu sang and Pattycake sang
Patty cake patty cake baker's man.
Kongo sang bake me a cake and Pattycake
Sang patty cake as fast as you can.
Kongo sang roll it pat it and mark it
With a B and Pattycake and Lulu sang
Put it in the oven for baby and me.
Children sang the native first.
Ngoma sang mother New Yorker,
Tambo sang mother, mother as fast as
Rare and raised as you can your captive
Mother and father who broke your arm
Roll it pat it mark it with a cast as
You put it in the mirror aghast as can be.

RANDALL MANN

The Summer Before the Student Murders

Florida, 1990

Persian Gulf
Persian rugs
Gimme golf
Give me drugs

Psycho House
Walkabout
Mickey Mouse
Pulling out

Take a load
Take a loss
Mr. Toad
Who's the boss

Pitch a tent
Boy in blue
Boy for rent
Overdue

Sandy trap
Going rogue
Jockey strap
Come on vogue

Lie awake
Twist the knob
Turkey Lake
Gobble gob

Chippendale
Chicken fight
Killer whale
Killer night

EMMA BOLDEN

Departures

I bandaged my feet and changed my boots.
In his Toyota, he drove without the breaks
over city and county, roads rain-grayed into blue.
I bandaged my feet before changing my boots.
Blood couldn't stop me. In my hotel room,
I woke to windows indecipherable from sky.
I changed my feet. I bandaged my boots.
He drove his Toyota. Without him, I break.

Tina Chang

Vivid Isolation: A Ghazal

I lived in the past, coursed inside a tale in blood
Each fingerprint pressed into my false trail in blood

Wide open the doors had blown, when students lay down
on streets to claim a signature that failed in blood

Within my body, my father's race and speed bound
with fury, small wings, a boat bobbed in hail, in blood

I had a child I hid from family, called *One*
a name he scripted on his tongue, *Love*, called his blood

At night, I walked barefoot to another country
freed from my own conscience, found in kin, shared in blood

Shahid died and folded a book into a bird,
released it East, it floated on saffron-scarred blood

When does anyone arrive home, shoes off, coat hung,
through the door we walk, a refugee flagged in blood

It's done, a land tilled for you. Agha, your imprint
is a couplet, tandem illusion, prayer in blood.

WILLIAM WADSWORTH

World Gone Wrong

(title and italic lines taken from Peter Cole's translation from the
Hebrew of the 15th century Spanish poem by Shelomo Bonafed)

The mujahadin martyred for God
are glamorized in popular songs
and the spice market hums with profits
on a horde of golden tongues.

To bow to Mecca you look west
from the Valley of Kashmir,
where the locals drink Black Dog scotch
and in summer Indian beer,

and in winter the lavender fields of saffron bloom.
One hundred thousand
stigmata plucked by hand
will yield a scarlet pound

of the Dust of Prometheus, the brand sold
by the locals. The spice market hums,
and the prophet speaks the truth foretold:
the world is not what it seems.

Ships sail the market streets,
Horses like lightning streak the sea,
The flaxen cord shatters iron,
Water, like wood from a tree,

Burns, and burns a hole in the holy
books and ledgers of book-
keepers alike. The wind in the Valley
forgives every account for the sake

of this abundance, brings the monsoon
down from the Himalaya
to the green terraces of the Jhelum
where the waters sprung from the loins of Elektra

pour down the Rapids of Alexander, steep and engorged
by the blood of Bucephalus,
to feed the purple fields of Pampore
and flood the floating metropolis

of Dal, where the waters turn to glass. They would,
if they could, stay forever here—fattening the peaches
and pears and plums in the orchards, making the world
a prophet can only preach.

PAUL MULDOON

from Frolic and Detour

The house wren, like the house sparrow
and the common spink,
is known to punch above his weight. Troglodyte, tinsmith in his burrow,
his *tink tink, tink tink*

bespeaking a familiarity with the science of iron-carbon alloys
the Chinese developed alongside the Dao,
he's believed to anticipate the lice
that will infest his nest by stitching into

its brush-pile the egg-sacs of lice-eating spiders. The going had been firm,
it's also believed, till government agents broke the seal
on the clouds over Max Yasgur's dairy farm.
Robert Lowell, writing of Thomas Merton's career in *Commonweal*,

praised it as "varied and spectacular," his own tendency to power-grab
implicit in that phrase. Toil nor spin, Bobbie. Spin nor toil.
Lowell knew that to be the center of attention is to be the crab
at a New England crab boil,

yet he would be sad, surely, to find himself bringing up the rear
to Robert P. Lowell of Virginia Tech, a research pioneer in the huge sulfide-
mounds thrown up around ocean-floor vents. Though it's rare
for me to deviate

from the task in hand, as I drove by Saugerties I noticed how Bill Graham
is even now obscured by a Marshall stack, despite his having lined
up the dairy farm's *crème de la crème*—
The Who, Jimi Hendrix, Joe Cocker. I marked, too, how the lark and linnet

sing their psalms
in *dán díreach* whilst mine represent a departure
of sorts. One exhibition I really must catch in the Iroquois Indian Museum
at Howe Caves is "Walking the Steel: *From Girder*

To Ground Zero." O-du-na-mis-sug-ud-da-we-shi ("makes a big noise
for its size") is the Ojibwa term for the house wren that builds in a bucket,
an abandoned bee-hive, a hangman's noose,
leaving on the lintel of each that time-release packet

of a spider-cocoon. When Tamenend, the Delaware sagamore,
shows up like a glitch
in the plot of *The Last of the Mohicans*, he leads us through the mire
and points us to a clutch

of five porcelain eggs with ferrous
speckles and splotches. *Vis-à-vis* scrap metal haulers like Saccomanno
and Vanzetti, I'm quite disinclined to theorize
on how they lost their business acumen,

preferring to withdraw to the spa town of Sharon Springs
and fill a dumpster hired from Fred's with cast-off drapes and drain pipes.
After the success of "Wild Thing,"
the Troggs are set on another "fucking number one." Spin nor toil, Bobbie.

Toil nor spin. In 1677 Kaelcop, clan-leader of the Amorgarickakan,
had sold the site of Saugerties for a piece of cloth, an English sgraffito jar,
a loaf of bread, a shirt. In 2017 we might throw in a bargain
set of three Adirondack chairs,

a tin pail, a Black and Decker belt-sander,
and the first paperback edition of Nancy Isenberg's *White Trash*.
A bird spotted recently in the environs of the Walmart Distribution Center
is the elusive Bicknell's Thrush

while American robins hang out at 204 Main,
the restaurant where Norm Phenix goes out of his way to wrap
Medjool dates in temptingly thick-cut bacon. On the *Spanish* Main,
meanwhile, Captain Hook lets rip

from Disney's *Peter Pan* of 1953. I'd just as soon not be sidetracked
by further allusions to popular culture
but the missing component, the "fucking fairy dust" the Troggs
will "throw over the bastard," is surely of a piece with Tinker Bell's glitter.

PERSONA POEMS

The thrill in writing a poem using a persona (a word derived from the Latin "mask") is to assume a mask different from your own and to channel that other via a new diction and stance on the page. Imagine becoming an actor and playing the role of another character. When you write a persona poem, you can shed your skin and enter the psyche of someone else. There are many sources of inspiration for persona poems—you can discover a speaker from a different time, gender, place, or culture. You could choose a person from biography, fiction, fairy tale, or film. The possibilities are limitless as you even could decide to write from the perspective of an animal or a plant.

There is an immediacy in employing the first-person pronoun in a poem which allows you to tap into a deeper emotional reservoir. By adopting another's point of view, you liberate yourself to utter things you may not say in your own voice. William Butler Yeats's most passionate love poems are spoken by the female personae he creates in his song cycle of the Lady, the Lover and the Chambermaid, while Langston Hughes' "Mother to Son" illuminates the perspective of an aging mother.

Through such acts of poetic ventriloquism, you may locate what is unique in your own voice. Your self does not need to be eliminated but may be expanded beyond where most writers will venture. It is possible to learn more about your voice on the page by assuming the mask of another.

John A. Nieves

Buckle and Wash

Holland Island, MD, c. 1913

When father rose to take to boat, he saw me
wrapped in restless sleep on the living
room floor by the window. He shook gently

my shoulder and wiped my child
tears on his coarse sleeve. *Was your bed
too soft, Mary?* I did not know I had uncovered

myself and slipped from my room. The floor
was cold enough to tell me I had not been
there long. *Papa, I had an awful dream.* I told

him I saw the ocean slink across the wooden
boards right where I lay, how it grabbed hold
of the walls and pulled them a-sea, how before

that, from the window, I could see a storm
and no town, no church, no graves, just waves
in every direction. Then the house fell, I dreamt

I floated over the roof, just hidden
by the bay's lapping. The sun came and strange
boats full of strange folks held cigarette

cases in front of their faces like they could
see me through them, then sped away. Leaving
only me here: the city silted, sifting. I spoke

solely through the croak broken in a gull's throat.
My father carried me back to my covers, kissed
my head and pointed passed my pane: *The water has*

enough. It does not need our town. But I knew
our ground would not be faithful
to the sky.

SEBASTIAN BITTICKS

From My Lord's Estate, I Pass High Mountains, Winding Streams, Rocky Torrents, Thick Forests, and Tall Bamboo

After Xie Lingyu (by Liu Songde)

Mine is the blind road. I sense a way by rote
sometimes guessing at the bend, knowing the mountain
for its weight at my side. Here or there my Master,
overcome, will doubtless pause upon the monk's hood,
or run a finger across mossy seams invisible to me,
but I move along. Mine is the pre-dawn. I meet
the watercress forager, crowned
with watercress. I hear the millstone lilting creek-side
devotionals. I bow beneath the laden millet
gold at dawn. Below a magnolia
that grows through stones of the field wall,
I pause at last to make my account on fingers black
from late-night transcriptions. My master's heart overflows
with ten-thousand sensitivities, but I've space only
for a list twenty matters long. Secret-footed,
I lay plans for his wanderings. I soak my sleeves
sweeping grasses from his path.

JOAN HOULIHAN

Sole Heiress

To Mother's silver service on a tole tray.
To the sprung Eros in her damask.
To the glory of Father's brass cuff-links
And trouser hangers.
To the hymns with gilt edge.
To the bible's pressed-to-death pansies and moth.
I am made like an icon: by looking.
Father? Yes. Mother?
Small birds fly out of her robe.
She has worked her eyes from behind.
A beautiful contrivance moving room to room
She comes to me like illness.
She proffers her artificial leg to match
My real one.
No doctor could explain her.
Born into a system, I outlive her.
My eyes, hands, and ears triumph.
In Father's name only, I establish
The saddest silver island in Germania.

RAVI SHANKAR

Laloo, the Handsome, Healthy, Happy Hindoo

That was my stage name but pure misnomer
because of my twin brother, that wrinkled,
parasitic, brainless mass of cock and balls,
who sprang sudden boners and who tinkled

when I was out in a tuxedo, trying to impress
the rich bodices and bustles out for a laugh,
that cutaway jacket with his gleaming watch-
chain eager to indulge himself in a penny gaff.

Attached to my shoulders, sprung misshapen
from my stomach, he was me. A living tumor.
Yet in medical textbooks, *I* was the monster?
He was not me, but living proof of the rumor

that Allah has a cruel, vindictive sense of humor.
I was not even Hindu but Muslim, from Oudh,
the second of four siblings, discovered by George
Gill, a British opportunist, who misunderstood

me as a freak to be exhibited in Germany. Sent
on a steamship *The City of Berlin*, the fastest
Atlantic liner, I was next sold to P.T. Barnum
to tour with the eclectic and certainly, vastest

"Museum, Menagerie, Caravan & Hippodrome"
known to man. I was family, if you can call
it that, with Camel Girl and Dog-Faced Boy,
my damaged brother draped in a Punjabi shawl

to appear my bride. He became my great pride,
my greatest shame transformed. I *chose* to stay,
even embraced my name, because I was a star!
Unique, a god who the common folk would pay

handsomely just to stand around. They marveled
at me, while I was busy forming an advocacy group,
the *Protective Order of Prodigies*, which, for a time,
convinced the circus and its dire fans that to stoop

to call us freaks was beneath them. Didn't last,
but I have no regrets. I even would do a side gig
letting doctors examine me. Ended up marrying
one of your kind. My personal fortune grew big

as a dirigible. Then the new century turned.
I was raking it in, touring the coast for Norris
& Rowe, when the sleeper car I was riding on
derailed. *Pulvis et umbra sumus*, wrote Horace,

we are but dust and shadows. That fateful day, five
flat cars were crushed to smithereens, six sea
lions squashed, and only young Frank Lentini,
then just a three-legged boy, survived. Not me.

31 years young. Still I had seen more in my life
than the entire succession of Nawabs of Oudh.
Was I happy? Healthy? In the end, only my blind
and mute brother can say. I lived! I was viewed.

MARILYN NELSON

Pity Eyed

At this rate I should have stayed in rehab
instead of getting dropped off at Walmart
to wait and wait and wait and wait and wait,
and Chris not showing up. So much for love.
So much for promises. So much for trust,
for what a man whispers to you in bed,
and you stupid enough to believe him
like your mama believed the man who left
her high and dry as me at Walmart now,
walking up and down the shiny lit aisles
of stuff I could use if I had a place
to use stuff in, checking my phone again,
nodding off in a booth in the snack bar,
pity eyed by the colored girl cashier.

ELIZABETH MACKLIN

This River

I'm 50 million now
and yesterday,

50 thousand years ago,
your people came

to live by me,
to live and stay.

My source is in the mountains, 100 creeks
join in my orography.

You chose me as the temple
for your goddesses:

at first I thought the Earth herself
chose you for me.

The hills still gather rain
to send me, over falls.

The properties of water
Earth conceived, including clouds.

As creeks come in again from left and right,
at that black hole where you couldn't play

or, above it, the ford for crossing borders—
south to north, clandestine, left to right—

once, your freshwater sirens beat at the water
with sticks, and the water leapt aside.

Farther down: the hornbeams,
where I move more slowly.

A hundred years ago
the water rose ten feet.

The water rose twelve feet.
I took out the bridge and saved the people.

Now here are trout, ferns; crayfish,
river rat, bamboo; new arrivals.

Here was your water mill. Now the mill mills
for the miller, who makes corncakes.

Although, farther down,
where I change names,

everyone does—still—speak of
the lamiak, freshwater, eternal,

who came all the way
from the ocean

under this same stone bridge
like the salmon.

Once your stonemasons were up to here
with so much salmon.

As we eat so will we work,
they said in the quarries.

Dams meddled with my liberty,
the salmon remain downstream.

But here right now you take advantage of my properties
even now, where the water goes salt.

It's always cured the itch.
You do like that.

Dailiness was what I was for you back then.
Or weekliness, every seven-eight days

clean wash rinsed clear,
then taken home to dry.

When you first lit the out-of-doors
I lit the out-of-doors, and paid the consequence.

Canals or turbines took my breath away.
I would have liked fresh water, hand to hand.

Yet here when I go down straight between your walls,
you do still continue to dance on either side of me.

By the sea the mountain rocks
have turned to sand.

Here where the factories came
you count my fish.

Now only fishermen care,
and those who need the water.

You could stop and ask them all
for how many quarts to wish.

At one time, you even sang to me.
Waiting for us down there is the sea.

JANUARY GILL O'NEIL

Sparrow

So let me be.
   Leave me
in this driveway puddle

to preen myself.
   Let the day envelop me
in its redemption

as the rain ends,
   lifts its cloud-skirt
to reveal the bluest of skies.

I earned it,
   sheltering under
leafless branches

and pitched roofs.
   My little bird-soul
deserves your praise

and envy. Watch me
   from your window.
See how I flit and splash

in your concrete pond.
   There is no known sound
more exhilarating than

my own heart beating
   against my chest—
breaking in waves.

I shake my feathers,
        sing only for myself.
What a glorious sparrow

I am.

KIMBERLY GREY

The Language of the Bomb

[I promise I am not certain, of violence I am,
eyes on the sun, more tender than memory,
less tender the more, I've had so many
hands, reached for submission, *they* stared
they started *they* tried, it's all in the *they*, a
pronoun will obliterate you, the hands of
others can, crater a life, keep your eye on
them, I am an exaggeration, no exaggeration,
of pre-existing dread, just the idea of me, like
Emily said, (*they* like to get the hurt in there,
like lawful poets) "*and yet—Existence—some
way back—Stopped—struck—my ticking—
We cannot put Ourself away,*" believe me
not my function, earlier before *they* came,
the flowers looked great, the ground, I was
not infinite with sound, I found nothing
sweeter than sitting quiet in my life, unlit
and unused, because you know, in war, *they*
kill me too]

LAURA KASISCHKE

Rescue Annie

CPR Doll

As silence, I carry inside me
wet, white ashes. Smothered
school bells. Swan at the bottom of the well.
Thunder under a mountain of rain-soaked party dresses.
The unperformed caesarean section. The small town slumbering
under an avalanche. The sound of the struggle ending
without a sound. Psalm
stuffed into a sponge.
Unrequited lust.

And still the little protest, little dream. Votive offerings. Wind
in a few streaming branches of a tree. Mistress mine. Never

not to be. A fish
stuffed with feathers. Bird
full of sea. *Paris. I was in love. It was 1880.* Twin Lakes, 1983, I was
a camp counselor infatuated with an EMT. *Haul*

*me out of a trunk, toss me on to the classroom floor, kneel
down here, and resuscitate me.*

(Sweetheart, sweetheart, does it hurt?)

(Of course it doesn't hurt.)

Mine, the most-kissed face in the world
Mine, the death-mask of the Seine's unknown girl.

DAVID YEZZI

One Hundred Umbrellas

After so long, I've finally arrived
exactly . . . where? Well, *here*. Yes, here, for sure:
a lampless street, an obscure neighborhood,
outside the walls, an hour's walk from town.
I gave up town. Now what do I have left?
A tiny dolor I've fed on for decades—
this pang is now the full scope of my gift.
But thankfully that's nothing at all to you.
I'm so glad you're here. You're good to come.
I've been turned down before, yes, many times,
by women who could clearly use the money,
artists' models mostly, like she was.
That dress you're trying on should fit you well.
It's stolen from the Ballets Russes, a getup
that Bakst designed for *Boris Gudanov*.
I took it last night from the costume shop.
It's possible I'd had a bit to drink.
Did I tell you that I'm writing ballets now?
Me and Picasso. Yes, and Jean Cocteau,
that imbecile. So earnest and effete.
Pablo's more my taste. He's *dee*-vious.
And yet his sets—of cardboard!—Cubist, so . . .
well, striking in a nonsense sort of way.
His kind of nonsense, though, makes too much sense.
Perhaps you'll come one night. We'll go together.
                    And, please don't worry,
with that screen between us, you can be discreet.
It's Japanese. Do you admire the work?
Indoors, it's cherry trees; outside, it's snow!
And freezing rain, then, finally, merely rain.

Rain.
            Sleet.

                    Rain.

Gray water threads the jet-black paving stones
in rivulets around the egg-shaped cobbles,
then back together and apart again,
before joining with the torrent in the gutters,
churning downhill like springtime in a valley.
Have you been to the South? One day you will,
when you are older. You will love the Alps.
You think I'm joking, but I never joke.
I sometimes smile, though that's by accident.
Occasionally, back when she was there—
the one I mentioned, Suzanne Valadon—
a smile would cross my face like a spooked bird,
for a second and then vanish, registered
only by her surprise, a passing shade.
The things I say must seem quite strange to you,
but I am not a madman, nor this a hoax.
It's just the way I am, a little . . . *what*?
It's true: I only like to eat white foods:
eggs, sugar, shredded bones, and certain fish
without their skins; fat from dead animals,
chicken cooked in water, moldy fruit,
rice, turnips, sausages in camphor, veal,
salt, coconuts, white cheeses, cotton salad.
I boil my wine and drink it mixed with fuchsia.
I love to eat, although I never talk
at mealtimes, lest I suffocate myself.
I breathe with care, a little at a time:
all that she knew.

Sleet's ticking at the windows. Sleet and ice
are not my elements. I prefer rain.
It rains in Paris in the key of D.

You see this painting? I was younger then.
My hair was long in back, and I affected
a stovepipe hat. I think that was the happiest

I've ever been. Spring 1893.
You see how foolish she has made me look.
Biqui, I called her. *Bonjour, Biqui, Bonjour.*
She painted it when we two lived together.
In separate flats. And I would play for her
a song to say good morning through the wall.

The rain has made a lake of dirty water.
There's black and then there is blacker than black.
There's nothing mystical about what vexes me,
but, at night, I play it over in my mind
eight hundred times (but first, an hour of quiet).

I'm boring you. Please, will you have a drink?
I think I will, if you don't mind. Absinthe
is just *anise* plus poison. Light through fog
calls home the small boats from the storm-tossed sea.

                    I know this place
is not so tidy. I had to fire the maid.
She made me itch, a very haughty person,
very arrogant. I always felt her eyes.
But you don't judge me, do you? No, my dear.
You are an angel, heaven's purest creature.
I'm not a slob; I just can't part with things—
magazines, newspapers. I've kept a record.
Here's April 13—there was an eclipse—
the last night that we spent with one another.
We'd been to see the show at the Grand Palais.
She jumped out the window when she left me.
No one will think of me when I am gone.

You're wondering at these umbrellas, my dear?
I admit they look quite frightening at night.
I find them on my trips into the City.
Sad creatures, wind-wracked birds with broken pinions

lying in gutters or crashed onto the quay,
or under porticoes in the Marais.
A few still work. This one is cut bamboo.
Its slender bones expand to lift its wings
against the midday sun or cold spring rain,
like the one we have tonight that won't let up.
After, you'll take it as a souvenir.
I miss the City, but way leads on to way.
These wounded dinosaurs are my mementoes,
like a tune of 18 bars ad infinitum,
because extinction sounds like that,
played over just the same each time, forever.

I walked to town today. I like to walk.
And now I have a blister on my toe.
I saw no one and yet it felt like home,
a ghost in purgatory, cleansed by fire,
while here I am in hell.
The markets of Montparnasse, the sculpted gardens,
the people to-ing and fro-ing on the stones,
a tussle overflowing the café.
Ha! Such wildness. Here, we have the rain,
a drip, a drop, a hovering mist of gray.
I worry that we'll meet around a corner.
I see her dressed in black outside the church;
I see her disappearing down an ally;
I see her in a taxi going by,
behind the high glass of an atelier,
nude, posing for her lover, or she's painting
in the sun of Montmartre in the afternoon,
in that same square that she knew as a girl,
growing up without a father, in the streets.

I also keep this canvas—by a friend,
the painter Santiago. This is me,
the blur at the piano; she is vivid,

her white cheek—ah, god—and her chestnut hair.
Santiago called the picture *Romance*,
damn him, the little fool: not a romance
but Gehenna. It's true: I hated her.
I hated her, not loved her, at the end.

The umbrella is a devilish machine, each one
as if flown from the blind recess of history
to die in a heap on the Pont Neuf. Or sometimes:
I steal them from cloak rooms when the staff
are smoking cigarettes outside in the alley.
I can't resist my lust for gorgeous things.
Look: this one has a mallard's head. How fitting,
a duck in a downpour, beads on its back.
The streets tonight are filled with mercury.

       Here's to you.
You see the fairy dancing in the flame
in green chiffon, like one of Degas's dancers?
Absinthe is a green fairy, so they say.
She's cold and growing smaller every year.
I hate her. I adore her. Her white skin
is the latest inspiration of Degas.
She often takes her clothes off for him now.

When you are dressed and ready, you may
behave as cruelly as you like, the crueler,
the better. Though, in truth, she wasn't cruel,
not wantonly. She didn't mean to be
uncaring toward me, though she never loved me.
That much I know, and when she realized
that it was so, she never came again.
She left a shelf of things: perfume, a brooch,
a snake with ruby eyes—a gift no doubt—
this portrait of me, and this satin dress.
I confess it is no costume. It was hers.

The one your wearing now. Come, let me see you.
One minute while I take away the screen.

O worthless idiot: she left no dress.
No, that's not it. I am not mad. She's here.

So beautiful.
Perhaps you'll come again tomorrow night?

Or stay a while, at least until it stops,
the rain. *Shh.* Listen, like a song. You'll stay.

        Rain.

Rain.

MYTH POEMS

Myth has played a powerful role throughout the history of literature. From Homer's *Odyssey* to *The Bible* to Ovid's *Metamorphoses* and beyond, writers have had an abundance of material to excavate. Myths from numerous cultures—such as Native American, African, Chinese, Icelandic—also offer sources of inspiration. You can reinvent stories that have been contemplated for centuries, re-envisioning a myth from the perspective of the present day.

Delving into these sources of mythological material allows you a shortcut into the story, sparing the necessity to describe the narrative. The title alone can propel you into understanding the underlying urgency behind the poem; the name Orpheus conjures many associations, as do Medusa, Eve, or Daedalus.

Poems which tap into mythological material can be both specific and archetypal at the same time. They also reconnect us with what it was like to experience certain sensory things during our childhood, as many of us grew up reading or being told these stories. Knowing Greek myths, inside and out, for instance, may be part of your pantheon and your vocabulary. When writing a poem inspired by myth, a poet can decide to set it during its customary era, replete with historic details, or resuscitate it anachronistically, as Rita Dove reimagines the myth of Persephone and Demeter in her book *Mother Love*. Poets sometimes even create new myths, as James Merrill does in *The Book of Ephraim*. The possibilities of mythic transformation are endless.

MARTÍN ESPADA

The Love Song of the Kraken

Listen to the love song of the kraken.

Conquerors sailing the world mistake my body for an island.
They navigate into hurricanes and blame me when the ships vanish.
They hurl harpoons at my bulbous head as I slumber in the water.
They say I crave the crunch of oars and planks, peg legs and bone.
They say I am a monster. They say I am a squid. They say I am a myth.
When I fade into the sea after the shipwreck, no one calls my name.

Oh, listen to the love song of the kraken.

You snarl at the gawkers who stare at us strolling on the boardwalk.
You drowse in the embrace of my tentacles as I dangle off the couch.
You listen when I tell the epic kraken tales going back a thousand years.
You kiss the trail of the harpoons and scrub the barnacles off my head.
You call my name when the sea takes me. You sunbathe on my island.

Yes, listen to the love song of the kraken.

Show me the armada of your enemies. Show me the admiral
in his admiral's pointy hat, leering at you from his spyglass.
Show me his babbling shipmates. Show me the sailor trembling
to light the fuse and fire the cannon. I will whip my tentacles
around their ships, hauling them to the murky bottom of the sea.

Let the insomniacs sedate themselves by listening to the whine
of whale song. Tonight, listen to the love song of the kraken.

CHRISTOPHER BAKKEN

Assos

They would rise, the islands, enormous beasts
somehow moving faster than our ship.

They hid their faces from us, but their backs,
covered in a coarse fur of thorn-bushes
and clots of purpling thyme, would seem
to heave as they swam, pull us to their shores.

These were not the Ithakas we wanted,
yet each morning we docked for a while,
if we found a harbor, so some of us
could be discarded. We watched ourselves dissolve
to distance in the ship's arrowing wake,
lines of us trudging up island-spines
in search of water or sheltering caves.

So we grew lighter, every day riding
higher on the waves. And so we had more time.

In the galley, we feasted on our grief.
We'd spent all our lives by then, had nothing
left to decide, beyond which one of us,
last hero bound for home, would steer the empty ship.

Duane Niatum

Sleeping Woman

She was a woman who fished in dreams for herbs
and plants on the healing path.
The village children last saw her at the mouth
of the Dungeness River.
They were watching salmon return from the sea.
The elders said she was the salmon's guardian
and when she sang they would leap as if calling her name.
The children round-danced and stepped lighter than joy.
Sleeping Woman, whom they met on the river path,
promised before the next rising sun she would sing
to them of a forest flower that smelled
of mystery, family and seasons, yet remained
a secret of earth and forest.
Her song flowed through the hollow of their bones.
The children felt larger than life and leaped
into the sky with moon moths.
Sleeping Woman, stepping softly beyond them,
veered in and out of light and dark and cedars,
disappearing in the rolling-back wave of the moon,
a deep swirl of planet and star.

JOHN A. NIEVES
Composition

Habits come from somewhere. When I was ten, a girl
in my neighborhood went missing looking for her
cat. The parents quickly assembled a search. My first

impulse was to look for my cats (who never went
outside anyway). Then I went back to my room
to watch from my window in case she emerged

triumphant from the woods, kitty in arms. I had
been reading about Bastet earlier and I remember
imagining the missing cat as a goddess off on a mission

to protect the sun. I'm not sure the police ever even got
involved. By sundown, the parents had returned
with the girl and the cat. My dad said no one should be

surprised if when you let something out, it runs
away. I didn't know if he meant the cat or the girl. Later,
my mother told me the cat found the girl a few streets

over and she went to the first house and asked them to call
her mom. This seemed riskier to me than running away.
I was pretty sure people killed more people than cats

or loneliness. Bastet first protected the sun, then ruled
the moon. Both girl and cat were lost then they were not.
Whenever something important to someone else goes

missing, I check to see if mine is in place. I'm not sure
what this says about me. Earlier I was reading about Anagolay,
the goddess of lost things. She was born of the seasons:

the passage of time often marked by the moon and the sun,
often marked by our memory of the moon and the sun, of writing
down where things were, where things are.

STEFANIE WORTMAN

Transit of Venus

Last summer the morning star
played a rare celestial role,
going a-progress as queen of love
through that million-watt follow spot
of knowledge, posing as beauty mark
on the sun's radiant cheek.

Now she appears before dawn
in more mundane formation,
rocking in the lunar cradle,
and the baby who debuted in summer
wakes and falls asleep again
in the still dark hours.

I listen for news about politicians
listening for higher news about the gross
domestic products of rape. They know
gods will what they will. Apollo bends
the heads of horses on their overheated
round and Zeus rains semen down.

The only will directing me now
is the unconscious one lodged in this
sleeping creature, wild like a man
just emerging from his monkeyhood.
Is she the goal of Venus' primping?
They say the Milky Way began as spray

from Hera's nipple when she nursed Hercules.
I thought it was a myth, but sometimes
when she feeds, my baby has to blink
her eyes against a shower of milk.
Then she draws back and punches me
in the tit like a girl ready for twelve labors.

Leah Umansky

Made / Maeve 1

After Westworld

1.

She was made, Maeve.

She knows the difference between men and gods,

what triggers, terminates and stuns.
"I thought you were all gods, but now I see you're just men."
      I type *my* into my cell phone. *"Maeve"* it auto corrects.

      We are similar creatures. We thrive. We must. We must. We must.
      The whole world stranges us, romances us, but nostalgia for what is
      ahead, for what is besides this, for what is before, is drowning our
      misery. We bruise. We makeshift. We dash. We dull. We savage. We
      tame and we take the tame out.

      We are both looking.
      We are both looking for a way...

2.

She creates her own story   a way   waits for the men to come.
She waits for the men to come   and stories.
She doesn't know anything about the world   but she designs herself to reach.
She knows the parts of her design.

3.

She says, "I can be someone else's problem," and is happy to be.

      We all want to be someone else's problem. I would be happy to be, but
      my softer misery is mine. I have fed it well. I heave my consciousness
      to its crests. The ocean of my tendering is a truth I workshop. I visit
      those dives. I plot those steals. I would bring the whole ship down.
      Maeve, her accuracy is a shared frontier. A promised land.

4.

Ford tells her, "you need not suffer; I'll take it from you" and I imagine the taking, the setting aside. I watch the feeling skim the prong, scraped aside, like meat from the bone. This wasteland, this game. This discovery of self. I was told, "you're okay. You're okay. You know how to protect yourself." And I do, but that doesn't make it okay. I'm not okay. My ability to protect is a poor tired dazzling. This is it, the spirialing inside me. The steeple of my hurt. The steel lit electricity of my heart. Imagine, if it were all not real. Imagine, if it were all removed, no turn for help, no turn for scrawling, or giggling, no turn for misspent days, years, hours. The fugitive in me, translated. What bright angel would matter that growth? What bright angel would take what is temporal, and dress it down? Who will take my suffering? I want someone to take my suffering. I want someone to take.

There are parts of us designed for better. We are a stare of stone, pleading to not be stone. A stagnant note unheard. A rise. A failure. This way to live, is not a way, it is a rise to fissure, storm or fall.

KEVIN PRUFER

The Damned

We could tell the saved from the damned
because,
           as the battle neared us,
the saved grew wings.

At first,
          they were barely noticeable,
two small lumps beneath a tight-fitting shirt,
invisible under a jacket.
               Months later, when the city's fall
was imminent,
            they'd grown large
and, even folded tightly,
              they poked from beneath
their coats,
          rows of neat brown feathers,
like owl feathers I remembered
from trips to the zoo with my father
                    in better times.

*

One owl, in particular, could turn its head
completely around,
            which astonished me,
though my father laughed at it.
              It's a trick
any owl can do, he said, walking toward the egrets.

*

He didn't live to see the newspaper photo
of one egret flapping its burning wings
over the smoldering zoo,
             or the enemy soldier
leaning against the ruined aviary

                              lighting his cigarette
and looking toward the smoldering ruins
of concession stands.

*

                      Anyway, that the saved among us
grew brown wings—some disheveled, some matted—
seemed like a mercy to me,

*

though it wasn't until the battle moved
right into the heart of the city—
                              not until
they'd burned the courthouse and filled the stadium
with the bedraggled and doomed—that the saved finally
took off their coats
                      and rose into the air—

*

my father would have been amazed
                              by their vast efforts,
their churning shoulders.
                      They must have seen armies
not visible to the rest of us,
                              though they called down no news,
hovering instead for several minutes
                              before, all at once,
streaming toward the mountains.

*

That was sixty years ago. For a time, we had traces of them
in giant feathers
                        discovered on the mountain paths—
though today no one gives them much thought,

so involved are we with the details of our lives,
we who have rebuilt our city
under the new administration.
                                Even the zoo is open again,
the new animals
                        bright-eyed and cared for,
busloads of schoolchildren
                                emptying into the exhibits
and gift shops,
                the clattering of strollers.

RICHARD TILLINGHAST

Shade

Is it not a fine thing
                    to stretch out in the shade of a cottonwood
even on a splayed and spring-busted old
                    couch like this one
and pluck the strings of a guitar
          while the slow river purls?

And now and then a trout rises
                    and the roar of the four-lane
is only a whisper
          over those copper colored hills.

And wasn't Jahweh himself
                    walking in the garden in the cool of the day
holding the book he was reading
                    open behind his lordly back?—
The Book of Love, let's call it,
because he was always eager to learn.

When he found them out
          he might have pulled one of his really nasty
                    Old Testament stunts.
But he stayed his almighty hand.
It could have been far worse for them
                              and for us.
Far worse.

"Without strife," wrote Hesiod,
"there is no greatness."
Even if strife means sunlight splintering
          outside the Gates of Eden,
                    the bruised heel, the dust of migration,
sweat pouring off your face—

Wailing, it is true,
      she, holding ashamed hands
         over her apple breasts.
He, while a snake slithers away through the undergrowth,
         gives out such a cry—
      speaking the first poem up toward the concealed stars—
as to be heard in the four corners
         of the newly made earth.

EDWARD HIRSCH

At the Expulsion

She was the sort of woman
Who looks good in a fig-leaf apron
And argues with you at the expulsion

She would not have been abashed
By a Voice walking alone in the garden
In the late afternoon shadows

And she refused to blame the serpent
For tempting her with the delicious fruit
Of knowledge nakedness good and evil

I swear she could convince the Lord Himself
To change His mind under a flaming sword
But she refused to give Him the satisfaction

I know too that Adam followed her willingly
Because heaven wouldn't be heaven without you

Eve Speaks

After you had named *leviathan,*
ziz for great bird, and called out *dissension*
for when the moon glowered at the sun;
creation for beginning, and *expulsion*

for the end, after you gave us *willow,*
thought up *oryx,* and what you tagged *tornado*
sent the *olive,* God's tree, trembling;
after the symbols—*almonds* for first love,

crocus for lamp glow—you fell silent,
because when you had found labels like *sin,*
archangels, heaven, even (God help you) *God,*
and each new phrase drowned in lion's roar

(or was it divine rage?), you declared *Enough,*
knowing you'd gone too far. Words can't give life
or raise the moon. And still I plead
Say my name, Eve. Say love. Say something. Anything.

EKPHRASIS

Ekphrasis is an ancient literary mode, first created by Homer when he described the shield of Achilles in his epic poem, *The Iliad* (approximately, 8th century BC). The writer translates the visual arts into speech. The trajectory of ekphrastic poetry extends into the 21st century where the static spatial arts offer a place of engagement for writers to enter into a dialogue with the art work or directly with the artist. An illuminating example of ekphrasis in twentieth century poetry is W.H. Auden's "Musée des Beaux Arts," a poem in which Auden contemplates how, in "Landscape with the Fall of Icarus," the ploughman and the sailors follow their daily routine oblivious to the tragedy of the boy drowning in the foreground of the painting.

The art of writing an ekphrastic poem compels the writer to push beyond the original source of visual inspiration. Often an ekphrastic poem will begin with sheer description, then veer off course, exploring other paths of inquiry. The art work, providing visual stimulation, offers another register of disourse. This exchange between the visual and the verbal arts can lend to intriguing collaborations. Paintings, tapestries, murals, movies, sculptures, photographs, statues, urns, tomb friezes, and buildings are some of the visual representations which inspire ekphrastic poems.

Vanitas

Look: the sockets in the skull
set on the table with a jumble
of other stuff—a pocket watch,
a mug, a manuscript, a candle,
a crumpled, stiff cloth hanging off—

can't see that the artist's palette
(whose vivid, skull-sized counterfeit,
heavy with great gobs of color,
is painted into a corner) has
a thumbhole in it like a socket.

Everything's inanimate
except the wit. On a false ledge,
brushes currently in use
are laid down nonetheless; top right,
perfectly intact, the canvas

is rendered peeling from its frame,
and dangling there is a self-portrait—
a little oval like a locket
ladies of quality once wore.
You ask the artist's name?

I can't read my notes here. All
I have is this picture in my phone . . .
It's Flemish, and I think on loan
from a gallery in (of all places) Hull.
Trust me, he's forgotten,

but isn't it wonderful, the skull-
palette with the black look of
an eye scooped out? I think I'd feel
great if I'd thought of that, at least
for a little while.

KWAME DAWES

Laundry

After Graciela Iturbide

There is something magical in the way the pillowcase
with its frilled lip swallows the wind and swells

beautifully under the raw network of electric
wires, how its fat gladness dances with her stained

but clean frock and the shirt she bought for him
in Panama City that Christmas years ago, all in this giddy

flop and swoop, the day working so brilliant at dawn,
as if this city will live on beyond the invasion.

FORREST GANDER

Terra Nova: Juno Gemes

Gossamer creatures in
a raw country of
mirroring pools. Held
in strangeness, in
a perceptual intermath. Their
postures—translations
of their own anguish, ardor,
asseveration. Bodies
breaking under
the weight of
epiphany. While sunset concentrates
its pastel
chromaticism. Only
slowly they will come
to see
the land, rolling away
from them
on all sides, is
already inhabited. There
never was
wilderness but beneath
the emotions
painted to their faces.
Always the signal
encounter has
already taken place.

MICHAEL COLLIER

Photograph of Two Young Couples with One Person Missing

They look much smaller when looked at
across the distance of thirty years or more
just as the rooms of childhood no longer fit
bodies that must stoop to enter their doors.

One of them wears an orange, paneled ski
jacket that will go in and out of style, another
a gray hooded sweat shirt, and the third a sweater
knitted by a mother who had never knitted before.

Only the ivy climbing up the trunk of an oak tree
adds green to the drab, wet day. One of the three
has died but you can't tell from the picture who he
or she will be. Each smile at eternity with equal conviction,

as if nonchalance was that moment's arrogance.
The two who survive go forward into a future
that shrinks as rapidly as they advance.
The brick sidewalk where they stood, ruptured

by roots, is now cement, and the one who holds
the snapshot, retrieved recently from an album,
wonders about the one who held the camera,
her whereabouts—such specific interchangeable lives?

Either they had just left the basement apartment
where the couple in the photo lived or they
were returning. The day was beginning or ending,
distinctions no longer important, except for the one

who is dead, whose whereabouts, there between
the living couple and the one who took the picture,
the one who became ex-wife before widow,
would never be in doubt, never be further than where

he was that day, in the middle of the going or coming—
all four caught in their unknowing futures.

GRACE SCHULMAN

Ascension

That morning, in the Church of the Ascension
on lower Fifth, once a sanctuary
for bonnets and top hats, I had a vision

of clipped pines, bamboo, a Kyoto garden.
Odd. In La Farge's painting above the altar,
Christ rises from the dead while his disciples

gaze heavenward, and angels swim in air.
Yet I thought pines. Perhaps with reason.
La Farge, his marriage ended, brushes dry,

went to Japan and gasped when he saw Fuji
loom over him. Renewed, he painted Christ
rising from the hills to heaven's kingdom.

But look again and see the Mount of Olives
change into Mount Fuji's snowcapped cone,
immobile, while a stream flows, an image

of what Lao Tsu called life's stillness and motion.
Now, in the Church of the *Ascension*,
I praise all things that soar and make a crowd

glance skyward: a wave of white thistledown,
an egret's dangling legs in flight; a siren-red
balloon; snow wafting high; a Buddhist's moon;

La Farge's Christ that turns into the Great Buddha
shimmering in bronze; and after that
Mohammed's horse; Elijah's chariot

let fly above the altar. I'll be there,
irreverent, a gazer, or perhaps
that is what sacred is, the work, the looking up,
                              the wonder.

LLOYD SCHWARTZ

Titian's *Marsyas*

The 16th-century Venetian master's very last painting—as big as life—is the story of the pan-piping satyr who dared to challenge a god.

Titian painted his crucifixion.

He hangs by his ankles from the branches of a tree, his goat-legs askew, as Apollo, kneeling, tenderly skins him alive.

Upside down, his tormented expression reads like a smile.

A thirsty pup is lapping up his blood.

Seated close—rapt—old King Midas, with his golden coronet, contemplates the horrific scene.

It's the 90-year-old artist's self-portrait.

Someone who's learned the cost of making art, the cost of challenging the gods.

And has accepted it.

Except for the glittering crown, most of the surface is rougher, murkier than the master's earlier dazzle.

Close inspection reveals paint smeared by his own fingers.

He put his whole body into this painting.

It was found in his studio after his death.

After how many years could anything still have been left for him to do?

A work is complete, Rembrandt said, if in it the master's intentions have been realized.

DAVID YEZZI

The Flaying of Marsyas

No one was much surprised when Marsyas
failed to outplay his rival on the pipes:
loud, upstart drunkard, fun until he's not.
They hung him upside down and set to stripping
away his skin—a grisly, painful death—
nailing it to a tree among the reeds,
the very ones his pipes were fashioned from.

Two genial butchers carry out god's will,
as they construe it, paring back the fur
below the waist and down where fur turns flesh,
as a fellow satyr stands by with a bucket.
A faultless spaniel laps the pool of blood.
The question as to whether Marsyas
deserved a punishment this brutal seems
not to have troubled anyone till after,
and then as an unspoken, fleeting pang.

Amidst it all sits Titian (dressed as Midas),
his chin in hand, observing every stroke—
as we do here in this dim gallery—
pondering at an unbridgeable remove
the flyblown odor of the killing floor.
Eyes heavenward, the fiddler has left off playing,
as if, instead of melody, a question,
never said aloud but thought, ascends aloft
the way that prayers fly up, to wonder at
what misdeed made the god so very angry
he stopped the feral pipes of revelry.

TESS TAYLOR

Notes on a Diebenkorn

Cityscape 1, 1963

How in him the light is primary—
high hard sheen of Berkeley,
eucalyptus hitting walls.
How his trick is catching
some refraction off the water,
a beveled salty mirror

forging afternoon.
The copper's shifty now
enough to tempt the fog in—

chartreuse & mineral asphalt
& a turquoise line—
foregrounded intersection

of gray perhaps-freeway
violet window// redstreak
mainlined from Matisse—

Color ecosystem; constellation
of not-quite location;
map at height or speed—

afterlife or foredream,
this blurred onrushing:

bright off-center longing
I always sense as home

CHRISTINA PUGH

Shirt Noise

When I first heard the phrase, I knew I would have to
unearth a poem called *Room Tone* in a book whose cover
shows an open picture window. An ice-colored
trapezoid pours against the glass. A woman in a partial
state of undress was not what interested the painter,
clearly—though the hair against her ear nearly echoes
the malachite, floe-like field that the window opens
onto and loves. I trust this woman. She's a pillar
sustaining what the painter wants to see. That wash
of blue rectangle—it might be a curtain, might be a net
to capture rays within paint. And how rosy the arc
above the woman's left breast. The rose of sex,
I know—its faintest intaglio. The window is a journey
away from the human. And how I'll acquaint myself
with room tone. Every time we record our voices,
we're told to hold our breath for five long
seconds so the engineer can capture the silence
in the studio, without any linen or cotton
or wool noise. What is the shape of that sound
I won't hear? The sere place our thinking rests upon?

KARL KIRCHWEY

Allowing That

after Marcel Duchamp's installation Étant donnés,
Philadelphia Museum of Art

Put your eye to the peep-hole in the barn door
      as many have done before you (the wood is shiny)
      and you will see, beyond the low brick wall of simile,
a prospect that is somehow familiar,

a place you visited once long ago
      that now accuses you: a pastoral
      landscape, a glistening tinfoil waterfall
near the town of Chexbres in the Canton of Vaud,

the whole thing touched by recollection's frost
      where the supine body of a woman
      lies nude, her legs spread, and the blind canyon
you thought you could traverse without cost,

the jagged grimace, this time refuses
      the gaze that pleasures itself to forget.
      You wrote her name in semen on black velvet—
do you remember?—though she has no face:

Veronica Franco, Simonetta Vespucci,
      Angela del Moro, Victorine Meurent,
      Maria Martins, Joanna Hiffernan.
Premise by premise, you come irresistibly

to a crime scene, and the gas lamp upheld
      in her left hand illuminates the evidence
      against you. By the last act of your violence,
she is Liberty Enlightening the World.

JUDITH BAUMEL

Hic Adelfia Clarissima Femina

In the catacombs of S. Giovanni, Siracusa

I want to look this way and be looked at this way.
Turned toward each other but askew, as if the planes
of our shoulders were made for different
vanishing points and still impose flesh
on each other's flesh. Me embracing *and*
presenting him, one hand draping a shoulder,
the other open across his upper arm. Both heads alert
but at rest, the way I find him in sleep
from another country, a momentary act of will,
crossing the border to seek that sheltering coast,
the smell of his skin under white Dalmatian wool.

As I will enter my niche alone, these vignettes testify
the thorny labor of marriage and its rare yield.
They testify as St. Paul preached here and Pelagius teaches.
Eve, eating in the Garden, is already covering herself
and Adam is guided from behind by Yahweh, present
in the breezy-time of the day. Good in Evil, Evil in Good.
When He damned the soil into which we return,
Yahweh gave us the mercy of pains in birth and bread.
Shadrach, Meshach, Abednego refused fear.
May my sons likewise be skillful in all wisdom to stand
untouched by fire, dew-washed and reborn as a shell.

AUBADES & NOCTURNES

Aubade

You have fallen into the arms of your beloved at night and lose track of time. The sun appears and, for whatever reason—or for all the reasons in the world— you must leave each other. An aubade, or dawn song, can be a love poem or a poem about the break of day. The classic example of an aubade is embedded in a dialogue between the lovers in William Shakespeare's *Romeo and Juliet*. Here is Romeo's rejoinder: "It was the lark, the herald of the morn; / No nightingale. Look, love, what envious streaks / Do lace the severing clouds in yonder East. / Night's candles are burnt out, and jocund day / Stands tiptoe on the misty mountain tops. / I must be gone and live, or stay and die."

The essence or subject of an aubade, as a love poem, often implies an illicit coupling of lovers who, because of daybreak, must separate. There is an implied counterpointing in the poem of being lost in the dark of night to each other and waking up to a world where the two must part. In this sense, the aubade contains both consummation and regret; communion and loss. Many contemporary aubades attempt to capture the transition from night to day, that in-between moment between sleeping and waking to a new day.

Nocturne

A nocturne, or night song, may be occasioned by dusk, those crepuscular moments as night arrives, but it also may take place in the dead of night, at midnight, or during the insomniac's *dorveille,* or may envelop an entire night, whereas, an aubade's temporal frame is more constrained, transpiring during those minutes as dawn breaks. Nocturnes arise from the darkest hour and plunge into the mystery of the unknown, often exploring what is hidden, the secret life. That liminal place between the unconscious and the conscious, the dream cosmos, can be tapped for nocturnes. This stanza from Wislawa Szymborska's "Four in the Morning" articulates the insomniac's plaint: "The hollow hour. / Blank, empty. / The very pit of all other hours."

Aimee Nezhukmatathil
Aubade with Wolf Spider

Hunger is the only spell, the first warning.
& you could say I wanted to draw it out

so mostly I drank water. I needed melty ice
to cool my tongue & teeth & was that hotel room

still lit this morning—lit all night long, really—
& were we really there? I left you before

your night-blooming jasmine crumpled
like a tissue & I wonder if you heard

its velvet song as you shuffled to your car.
I'm still on the curb, a firefly's forgotten little lamp.

Or I might be the wolf spider we saw in the orchard,
her back spilling over with her babies. No stonefruit

could sweeten that bit of pity we both held for her
in that exact moment. How I wanted to taste

your lips right then & I know some delicious days
I don't think of you but days I do will be full of thorn

& honey locust. How to say it? How to pray it?
I press the still-warm welts on my legs—the last ones

I'll have that summer—to feel their secret heats,
each bite a remembrance, like a souvenir.

DAVID BAKER

At Dawn

Is there no sound to   stopping is there no

stopping first at night   this fitful quiet

to waken now to   find such heavy snow

where was nothing trees   shattered and hear it

nowhere cloud landscape   of silence stopping

through the night my sleep   a dream of falling

beyond anywhere   you might be listening—

ELIZABETH SCANLON

Aubade

In the heaven of the martyrs everyone gets what they deserve.
For the rest of us, something more variable.
You snore, I obsess—each to their own worst traits and if
the debate leaves you unable to sleep for hours,
at least I get a head start. Often when dawn teeters
on the edge of the window and you are coming to bed as I rise,
the purple sky is the bruise of wanting:
it lightens quickly but I can still feel where
I've pressed so hard the vessels of night burst
beneath the surface. It may be we promised
all of our time in order to find any time at all,
net-fishing our chances to have some sort of life
together before the gains are weighed.
Let it be said, we deserve each other.

MAURICE MANNING

Canebreak Love and Water

A patch of light in the sky appeals,
meanwhile, a barn owl presides
from the top of the sycamore beside
the stream on its way to enter another.
Confluences of small degree,
a fiddle-tune in a minor key—
the rhyme occurs, naturally.
I observe the dim silhouettes,
the continuous reality
of morning when some are still asleep,
the barely seen and the quietly heard.
Love renews itself and keeps
beginning, as water waters the stream
and the stream's entrancing motion is stirred.

This portion of the world is like
a mind with the strains of a song in it,
allowing an inconclusive thought.
None of this needs to be finished now,
but I've enjoyed imagining
the canebreak following
the stream in still serenity,
a stiff presence pricking the air
for what was here originally,
in blades of green and greenish yellow,
the living thing in the living shadow—
but none of this needs to be finished now.
An art with something quiet in it,
and something that isn't even there.

Music for Attack Helicopter

The punch card skyline
from here to tarnation
as seen through a
      Summilux, darkly :
the power grid a scaffolded arbor,
empty billboards advertising
advertising space, gantry cranes
in the harbor a calyx of gaunt red
ideograms, chicken-scratch
commuter traffic blurring the
eyebrow bridge.
      I'm a dislodged
calque of liquid finance—
hellbent on making the Zürich
flight, at 5 : fucking : 30 a.m.
—in transit across a Minecraft
metropole is what I am. A cursive
crack in the windshield
of nobody's car.

MAI DER VANG

Nocturne for the Bereft

The spirits toy   with me.

        Their wooden hips
    Nudge me

      Into cypress fields.

       I begin to chant:

     I am no
     Longer rooted
At the helm.

   They cleave me   for days
    Until I am
        Nothing but string.

    I am their flimsy

    Heading into a new north,

   Collapsing at
The scent of jasmine

   Filling up the
       Jinxed hour.

I cannot   eat the reasons for
   An ochred smoke
Tiptoeing

Around me   night to dawn.

What about
The hand ghosting

Me from
Underneath the desk.

I yield,   limp through it all,

A tigress—
Damned,

Ill with temptation.

EDWARD HIRSCH

The School of Night

From up here
Dusk looks like a gray stream
Of milk poured into the valley

Daylight is lingering with the shadows
Like a teacher reluctant to leave class

While the saplings
Are pulling on black coats
Like students
Hanging around the yard
Under the lengthening purple clouds

The swifts
Darting through the air
Are erasures on a blackboard

The owl
Is a broken pair of glasses
Dangling from a high branch

A wind rampages
Through the leaves
And soon only predators
See through the blackening

No one is left to patrol the grounds
But an old man standing
At the rails
Gradually losing his sight
And peering into the gloom
As if it were a lesson plan
He's afraid to decipher

Because whatever it is
The night will teach him
He doesn't want to learn

LISA RUSS SPAAR

Expectation Nocturne

With the old same-ache—
as though we'd never yet—.
Or as if, one minute swallowing
the next, the next, the next,

interminably, after mute
but acute storm, the sky, wary spouse,
comes out, unlouvered
& wild with sorrow, aloom at dusk

over earth's broken dishes. I vow
to trust this secret blue, tunneled tugging,
wrapping fists around the rope,
O sunken Well, whose infinite hug

I cannot always fathom but whose weight, dram,
I believe, draw up, a word, a mouth, an omen.

STANLEY PLUMLY

With Weather

All day you watch the frost flare
into each end point of the star.
The cold is like glass on your skin.
You know if you sit here long enough
how brittle the body becomes.
Even the paling light is on two sides,
as you sit in the sun half, half sun,
the lie in your lap, filling your face.
You're like a man in love with something—
some word, a gesture, the one line of evening
lost among those trees, a man in a chair
watching it starting to rain a little snow.
You could get up and join the snow.
You could move to a warmer window.
You could move to the middle of the room.
You could get up and turn on the lamp.
You could sit here alone in the dark.

CALVIN FORBES

Rock Star

The TV off
The radio too
I took my son
Outside into
The backyard
Pulled open
Two lawn chairs
And said look up.
It was a night
Clear and dark.
I said to him
See up there
Those are stars.

ECLOGUES

The eclogue is a type of pastoral form in dialogue where, traditionally, two shepherds converse or sing, extolling the beauty of country life. The notion of a dialogue remains inherent in this form. In a more contemporary context, there is a sense of an argument or dialogue built into the eclogue. The poem may be spoken in voices or may contain several voices within one. Poetry inspired by nature can come out of actual rural experience or else, as an urban dweller, can arise from fantasizing about the virtues of rural existence. Writing an eclogue underscores the importance of the relationship we have with nature in poetry. Other types of poems inspired by nature include pastorals, bucolics, as well as ecojustice and environmental poetry.

Eclogue

Past the pasture where the mind goes grazing,
A drop of dew bends down the blade
Of grass. Peril there persists as the ever-present
Tense: the ant stalking the aphid
Steps on the shadow of each leg, the spider
Weaves in the air the pattern of its prayer—
A little death, just enough to last another day.
Breezes blow in that breech the void's far-reach
Carrying scraps of pages bearing the scent
Of other thoughts: *The clover leaf smells and tastes
as its flower.* Being a person is prison enough
To beg your brief parole. Release is no more
Than brief harm springing from the grass
Its odor's lock: a footstep in the field.
If granted permission, you can read the torn
Pages and gather what wisdom they yield—
Or, you who are your own warden—
There you can forget what it is to read,
To need some word not your own to make
For yourself a draftless home you cannot
Build yourself by yourself. There is no
Hammer in Arcadia. Just a heart that beats
Like a hammer. You know it as you know
In a dream all things, but waking you find
You know nothing at all—your creature,
Your heart, wandering so far within you
It has wandered away. Gone to meadow.
Gone to pasture. Knocking the dew
Off the blades. It laps its water
From a spring as blue as the blindest eye.
To find it find the path across abyss
That wears away the foot that walks it.
I think I've caught the sheen of green
Floating in the night sky, a simple square,
Some error of the telescope's lens,
The refraction of a star, in a picture,

In a magazine. I've also caught the scent
Of clover when in a dream my daughter
Turns her head and her hair spreads out
Across her pillow, like grass, like—.
The goat-kids bleat so softly in their sleep,
Dreaming of suckling in the shadows
Of their mothers. The goatherd forgot
The words, but gently pipes the tune—
No father, no mother, just the worms
That work the loam, oblivion's song
That holds the field together, you must
Learn to forget if you want to sing along.

SOPHIE CABOT BLACK

Forage

Out here solving for winter grass, words
Turn simple. Which is how it begins:

Aware that come morning, the missing appear
Or not. You wake into either side of what might

Have been heard, then discarded, and the pasture
Scarcely changed. Before, I could not imagine;

After, I cannot imagine anything else,
Except to keep the small alive. Sheep by sheep fed.

*

There are those who number their lambs
And those who paint theirs blue.

Loss marked down. Loss buttoned in
To a left ear or swipe of red at the haunch; the ram

Quivers himself off each ewe.
In the spindle of muted light the others

Do not look up: the low grass
In a song of rip upon rip, mouth by mouth.

*

All I have loved
I have loved alone. Cold is colder

Even as the North melts into the never
Before. I pay for all who

Already came; this field worked as far
As any can remember. Eaten down to root

I move from ground to ground
And back again. I move each animal and so move myself.

*

Tired of explaining my work; if I could
Reconcile the sheep I could change

The sheep. To convey the whole you must move one
By one; mark the lesser to keep off

From what they want. The compass does what it does
Which is nothing but find itself.

*

Beware the old gate: when opened it cannot be closed
Until all are through. The hungry pour out

To find the other side
Ruthless in new grass. Loosened onto plenty

Some will be made lame by much. The founder
Of each hoof quick with pulse and sudden blood,

Until knee by knee she walks: she cannot
Stand, the green traitored against her.

*

Starlight not for us to see by
Cannot ever be the reason. To keep the count look away

Enough to see any white
Against the night. Over and over

The ram bangs the slatted pen,
Each unencumbered sheep settles into her grief.

*

I walk the edge to lay the scent so the dog
Will not run off; I sleep when the fox sleeps. To be

The better shepherd is to make the field work
Wherever you go. Carried on your back

All you have known, removed until ordinary.
Sometimes the wind is wrong. How far to head

Before looking back. Some say turn around,
Others say not. Always the ground for both.

JOANNA KLINK

3 Skies

And sometimes sky, falling through scales of color,
lifts our eyes enough to see. A tree packed with starlings
explodes in spectral dawn. Rain breaks across a road
in curtains of seed-pearls. Your ear picks up a cry—
animal or man. What we have taken from other lives
flashes from black quartz and sifts through highway
mist dissolved by noon. Blink and it returns
in the blown glass of clouds, the cool threaded sound
of water running. Crushing beauty is laid every day
without scorn at your feet. On a black sea,
fields of stars are opening inside you.

*

Hammered copper. Heirlooms and winter photographs,
the deep wear of ore. There is no far country. You will know
to draw close to certain laughters, certain lights in the eyes
of men and women that blaze past their frames.
Whatever they touch is increased. They live past suffering.
Time of the great light of possession, ice and years.
Time of dust. Time of snow falling on roads.

*

In the ease of winds and sun, a fountain has sprung up
in you. An apple is falling. White light crosses
the grasses all day. Care of air, care of lives—
they are the same. No distance is empty. To stay here
always you would need another hour. You would need
to draw alongside the children, the blown roses, the dawns
and distant rains. Night ranges across the arable land.
We remain inside its purposes.

CAREY SALERNO

River Channeling in the Ear

River, what are you? Song of water too
pretty for the mouth, finger to scrawl.
Place we drink from, place we drown.
River above my head, daring to pour down
all the family secret, this invisible wet crown
where in the ear the words are chunnel and resound,
resound, and sound and sound, the dirty chamber
shutting the mouth, its levy, impound, its rain
hammering round a river above my head
making no sound, the secret in not ever out
bound, its bound, unbound. River, what are you?
River I drink from. River in which I drown.

ELENA KARINA BYRNE

Eclogue in Orange & White

Then *I say Thirst* sitting in a field, after
its orange light falls, drinking five glasses of childhood
milk at a time, as the *train moves . . . moves into fathomless space,*
unwavering the light staved from L.A., Munich to Paris, devoid of
personal instructions. Rain comes. *Rain can leave a person blind*
or in shadow. I wave my hands over my head, two more
hours, as if you were still here. I make amends with desire.
Your distances. Your grief rhythm. An accident

road is covered in salt, mouth in salt, and above the crows'
height of the sky, clouds are stacking their milk paintings.
Look at them. Far off and up close. Look down at
the mother walking over orange beach debris, sorting.
Even the constantly moving water turns orange: bright

accident. Here, *I prepare a few French sentences.*
For the cigarette I will never smoke. For the entire film
quenched on rain and darkness, implying a smell of oranges
swelling in the white viewing room. *While eating my sandwich,*
I ate one end of my scarf, bleeding its orange into my back. But
it will not keep me warm in this thought.

Because you are not here listening to me, as *so close*
once that I think I saw the pilot's face veering away
or my own, veering toward, bending over a glass
of milk and an unpeeled orange resembling fish skin.
Both of us made the ugliest gestures away from the sky.
Something then astonished and ripped open, burst
out, cut and bled for miles like a dell of body mud ditched
in the endless, dense, wildly fecund ice-grey, and to

myself, a long time ago, it was very hard, so post-haste. So,
I now bow, shout, white-knuckle it in the riddle drug of time
that took away the patience of parents and you. Every day said,
"Walk." But mobility scolds this cold. The cold bites back into
the horizon. Like a mother done and extruded from orange trees,

a father upheld, riding a war plane's ghost updraft, these
quiet botanical of words draining the light, de-assembling
its far sound from milk pouring down from God's ceiling.

I outlawed, for us, that force coming from inside
my morning, my night, my afternoon, my feet living
out their last season of grief. No two people know alike.
Loss, like a bicycle, is a *greasy soul* wheel out of a dark
cemetery coming towards you, inside, every day. As if
orange *apples pummeled the ground* around us, it turns
out, I walked the whole map's enclosures unending.

CHRISTOPHER MERRILL

Lines at Tongdosa Temple

Rain, and a fallen pine at Mountain Gate,
And soy bean paste fermenting in brown pots—
I bow to the monk surrounded by his work.

———————

Halfway across the Bridge of Liberation
I lose my footing on the slickened stairs
And nearly fall. . . . How to regain my balance?

———————

Sound of the origin, Heaven and Hell:
The drummers summoning the monks to prayer—
And then the wooden fish, the cloud-shaped gong, the bell.

———————

Tea and rice fields, a pond of lotuses
Past blossoming, new friends in an old place:
The trees spared by the occupying army.

———————

Lightning, thunder, and rain in Paradise
Hermitage, where the master taught. Idle
The earth mover by the new dormitory.

———————

Enter the labyrinth of sutras carved
Into ceramic tiles and stacked on shelves
Behind thick glass, and you may never leave.

———————

Persimmons ripen in the orchard, chickens
Cluck in the mud, green tea leaves steep in glass—
So many gifts from the venerable monk!

———————

The water wheel turns in the driving rain,
In the empty courtyard high up on the mountain.
Did I hear it right? This work is never done.

NATHANIEL PERRY

Earthly Love

Wild alarm we can only
just make out—a calling
out, a figuring.
There is no one lonely

world, it seems to say.
Woodpecker now in the crown
of a red oak is a stone
set briefly in the sky,

or an agent of agate, live
reminder of what is born
to us: beginnings, warnings
both urgent and instructive.

MAURICE MANNING

Yellow Time

I'll not describe the field it pleased me
to enter with nothing on my mind,
because nothing was what I needed
then at the moment of beginning.
Proximity soon mattered—I looked
at things a small distance away
and tried to keep a radius
of ten to twenty feet around.
I wasn't going for a vista,
I wasn't going for anything
at first—that was the mystical point,
to set out empty-hearted and blank
in the brain. I didn't have a thought
for several rounds around the field,
just being methodical and quiet
without a purpose. It was morning,
I was solemn in a happy way.
I was basically walking around a field
with an open heart and an empty mind,
and then there wasn't a heavenly voice
at all, but I saw the yellow yolk
in a daisy's face and it came to me,
it's yellow time, it's yellow time,
as though a gear in the year had ticked.
A lot of yellow was there to see,
it was easy to see it everywhere,
even the grass was tinged with yellow,
yet I had to admit I was wrong. I saw
it's also lavender-purple time,
there were flowers there to tell me so,
if you believe a flower tells.
And so I was admonished, yet drawn
farther into the dream, as if—

as if the prominent yellow flowers
and the lesser lavender-purple ones
had painted me into their scene,
and that's what I was going for.

APHORISMS

Imagine the aphorism as one of the shortest forms in literature, a chance to say something as succinctly and with as much punch as possible. As James Geary writes: "They are terse and to the point because their message is urgent. There's not time to waste. An aphorism can be anywhere from a few words to a few sentences long . . ."

We think about the aphorism as something particular and precise, but its definition is quite general. It can be viewed as a saying that is generally instructive. Beyond that there is a lot of elbow room. There is no exact perimeter of length or form, as long as we can glean some kind of lesson or viewpoint. The aphorism can be an epigram, a pithy maxim, a double-jointed chiasmus; it can even be contained within a longer poem, an excerpt that suggests some informative perspective with practical applications.

Writing an aphorism is a way to flex your muscles, a type of poetry calisthenics.

Jeff Martin
Intelligent Design

If life is a caterpillar
And death's a cocoon
How soon?

JAKE YOUNG

Aphorisms

To the grape, wine is blood; to the jaguar, blood is wine.

*

The quickest way to lose someone's attention is to demand it.

*

Books make grave robbers of us all; they are tombs from which we aren't afraid to steal.

*

The road to avarice is cobbled with discarded morals. It is an unsteady path, yet many travel upon it.

*

The longer I watch & contemplate the magnolias, the more I observe myself.

*

To resist capitalism is futile, but not to is feudal.

*

Do not be discouraged. Even unleavened bread receives blessings.

*

Time is a lie we set our watches to.

SOPHIE CABOT BLACK

The Handbook of Risk

Do not pull back so far
As to see too much

It never goes away:
Simply moves to another plot

What does not correlate
Becomes how to choose

If you name it you will lose it
If you have it you don't want it

Excess can only be known
When up against another

As you cannot manage
What you cannot measure

The strategy used today
Will not exist tomorrow

The original
Cannot be returned
To the bottle

The new will come again
And will not ever end

Seek out who will spread the pain
As eventually someone must pay

We keep saving
What should be allowed to go away

Absence of evidence
Is not evidence of absence

If you are not what we already have
Then we have made you what we need

The alchemy of building one
In order to produce the other

There is always somebody
On the other side

Give them a little extra
To run out just enough
In order to need again

More can happen than will happen

Being both long and short
Keeps you in touch with all gods

The machine has been structured
To hold what we want
To take place

The more we are connected
The more we know our black swans

When in the alternative space
Look for a high-water mark

Rushing in at the wrong sign
Rushing out at the wrong sign

It is until it isn't
Every time a different time

When we are certain of the outcome
Risk begins

Find the gap. Let leverage
Take you as far out as you can bear

Watch how the world moves
On one pivot, believing itself
Whole and worthy.

DAVID BAKER
Island Music

I had to hear it to see the tree frog—

*

Rain begins in the night   in the first night—

*

And the sound was like breathing, the island gathered close
around, scent of gardenia—

*

After the scavengers are gone, the white skull laughs.

EMMA BOLDEN

After the End

Left long enough, letters
will lose their patience, fidget,
exchange places until
Love evolves to evil.

Last Poem

Don't judge the rats.

We're all condemned.

CHRIS GREEN

Drinking Together

Perhaps the world ends here.
At a bar.
No matter what,
you are the wound & not
the medicine.

KARL KIRCHWEY

Pax Americana

(Juvenal Satires X)

An oak was standing half-split in a field.
        Milo the strongman, who was passing by,
        felt quite provoked by how defiantly
three wedges, driven deep, were being held.

He braced and set; knuckle opposed knuckle.
        The tree's red heartwood roused and spread and groaned.
        The wedges rang as they fell on the ground
just at the moment his strength chose to fail.

The trunk eased shut around its wounded cleft,
        leaving Milo helpless, trapped in it.
        Wolves browsed at leisure on each delicate part;
returning woodsmen buried what was left,

the gravestone of the man who was so big
effortlessly split by a barren fig.

PROSE POEMS

With a prose poem, you take away the construct that most identifies with poetry—the line break. After all, the definition of "verse" derives from the Latin, "versus," or the turning of the plough. In a prose poem the line runs across the page without a break, presenting itself as a block of print. Richard Howard writes about the prose poem: "verse reverses—the reader turns at the end of the line—while prose proceeds." How do you simulate the power of the line without line breaks? It is the sentence, instead of the line break, which becomes the guiding technical principle. The challenge of writing a prose poem is to retain the poem's heightening of phrase and the surprise of its language while the line remains limitless.

Think of the prose poem as a container filled with the unexpected. It is literally a poem contained in a box of prose. Its container are the walls, ceiling and floor of sentences. David Young suggests the different subjects for prose poems: "Life histories reduced to paragraphs, essays the size of postcards, novels in nutshells, maps on postage stamps, mind-bending laundry lists, theologies scribbled on napkins." A striking example of the prose poem is Elizabeth Bishop's "12 O'Clock News" where she describes the objects on her desk from an alien's point of view.

MARY JO BANG

One could say the train is resting

One could say the train is resting when it's stopped in the middle of the tracks. We're waiting for the lulling sentiment of forward motion, a love song woven into the wheels. *I love you, I love you, I love you,* woven into the wheels. That's the letter to the world she wrote. The frosted lampshade dials down its output, then emits a dreamy glow. To my left, a man's wearing a suit: coat, pants and tie. Anything I have on makes me one of any number of hopeful feminine heroines. *I wrote a letter to the world.* The swan is not only singing but also playing a harp. There's a humming circle of feathers at its feet. In the dining car, for luck, pinched salt is pressed tightly between two fingers, then tossed over one shoulder. Good luck with that. When I stand up, the suit folds his flower hands and closes his eyes. *Don't forget,* he says, *the spoils belong to me.* At that, the plastic raft at the center of the sea slides back behind a blast of wind. The wildfire makes a sunset blush. The seven people in the sleeping car, each in a separate berth, hold their collective breath. The story of obstacles overcome is being recorded with the economy of an index card. In the window's artificial eye, a perfect edge and a battered edge are battling for their lives.

MICHAEL COLLIER

The Salvation of America

Flagstaff, Arizona, 1972

Whenever I hear someone say we need businesses and corporations to solve America's problems, I think of Gene, our foreman, who drove a red, Ford Ranchero, and wore laundered Western shirts with pearl-snap pockets and cuffs, a belt buckle the size of Montana, where he was from, and round-toed cowboy boots. He smelled of bay rum and Brylcreem and waited in his cab for the dust to settle before he'd open the door. "Fuck" was his main form of encouragement and "I don't give a shit," his answer to everything *we* said about why the job was off schedule, and then he'd disappear for a while in the trailer where his Mormon bosses, who wore white hard hats like soldiers, chastened him with their calm, terrifying, alien demeanors. Gene was an employee of Ken Cail Plumbing who fired him, then the Mormons fired Ken, and all the rest of us were let go, including the welders from Lubbock. The rest of us: Ray Borst, John Likovich, a squirrely, acne-faced guy whose name I don't remember but who had dreams of becoming a classical guitarist, and Michael Collier.

Whenever I hear someone say *that* about American business, I see us standing in the deep, wide ditch blasted out of solid rock, meant to carry water, gas, and sewer lines, looking up at Gene, Ken, and the Mormons, with their sick, despairing, hopeless, not-really-knowing-what-the-fuck-to-do expressions, except to have the four of us, teenagers, pre-apprentice plumbers, with long, stringy hair, each with a shovel, to keep spreading popcorn-size volcanic cinders, wheel barrowed from dump-truck loads, to cushion the pipe, hoping, but not having a clue, that when the ditch was filled the lines would bear the weight.

Erika T. Wurth

Like a Polaroid / Faded

What's it like / what is it / I sometimes wonder. To hold them in your arms while they scream or slam their doors / the memory of their hair in your nose. Soft. Brown. Perhaps they come from your very body. Or the body of the one you love / loved. What's it like / what it is / I sometimes wonder. I knew for such a short time. There was an idea. It had my eyes, his hair. Black, but only in my mind / black, this hair, those eyes, like both of our grandmother's eyes, hair. Oh her Indian hands, so soft / I remember. This idea / this / tiny reality / oh god / so small. It looked like an idea and what I mean by that, is it looked like everything inside of me / everything that had ever been / like a Polaroid my father took / faded. The cruelty of this thing / the blood. And I mean it; blood / what I mean. This is not abstract, faded. It is a real thing that came out of my real body, very very. It was an ocean, bringing her out with the tide, the smell of her hair that had probably never been, the feel of skin that had barely just begun. What is it like / what is it, the blood. I tell myself things about this blood / this skin / this fading memory that has the opposite emotional life of the grief I feel for my father / as it gets worse over time. I say she wasn't meant, to be to be. I say it's not my path, this skin, that hair, that smell in my nose. That woman I see exhausted on the train beside me / I feel sorry for her / but not really / I feel pain, is what, I / feel. Once, right after / my little niece said: I believe / that the spirit / of a child / lives and decides whether to stay or go. Why / why did / she decide / to go, and if she did / where / god / does she live?

Gary Young

My body does not belong to me

My body does not belong to me. Lying motionless for an MRI, the magnetic coils grind away, searching for tumors. I imagine little seeds of death floating all around us. The hypnotic machine pulses and whines, and I'm in the monastery, meditating while cicadas electrify the stagnant air. A monk beats on a wooden drum, and the imaging machine speeds up. The monk whispers, still yourself, and the technician says, you're almost through.

SANDRA BEASLEY

Jefferson, Midnight

In another version of this story, he is a naturalist who dabbled in politics. He reinvented the plow. He joined the American Philosophical Society's Bone Committee and, while trying to prove the great Western lion, gave us our first giant sloth. He shipped a rotting moose to France to demonstrate the greatness of our mammals. He is a father of paleontology who didn't believe extinction was part of God's plan. He asked Lewis and Clark, should they encounter the mammoth, to capture one. For months his sea wall has been sinking, the Potomac's mudflats sucking at support timbers. In 1918 and for six summers after, the Tidal Basin was chlorinated so this bank could become a beach— Whites only. Those who are drawn to rising heat populate the ceiling of Jefferson's memorial. Once the sun sets, the temperature drops; they lose their grip and fall. Bodies bounce off my shoulders, bodies land in my hair. Guards call this the spider rain.

CYNTHIA MARIE HOFFMAN

Smoke When You Can't See What's on Fire

A fire burns somewhere off the road, and you are not you again today. In the distant sky, a bird has got hold of a fat grey snake of smoke and is wrangling it out from the treetops. Down below, a woman lies in the burning house where the bright tongue of the snake is lashing. Secretly, slipped behind a quilted bedskirt, a child's collection of feathers melts into wax inside its miniature cardboard room. You drive down the highway watching the wind rip the scales off the snake's body—bits of ash flickering against the sky. It's sort of beautiful. The whole mountainside catches fire in the sunlight. The bird lets go. You are not you again today, driving the road home, having taken the smoke with you. Having tied the smoke around your throat like a scarf you wear at night as you sleep, covering your ears against the angel who stands in the dark corner, saying nothing. In the forest, a child runs barefoot across the roots, her torn dress flapping behind her. A light flickers in the leaves. The child will build a new house starting with her one brick of feathers. You have a child, too, and she sleeps in the other room, dreaming her rough-pelted teddy has come alive. In the morning, she tells you she saw his bones in the x-ray machine and his beating heart. But inside his bones, there were tiny germs. As her mother, there is a gift you want to leave her with. And it is not this imaginary house built of ghosts. This worry. It's okay, she says. Baby Bear just needs his medicine. It's okay.

KIMIKO HAHN

Stop Me If I've Told You This

my father says before launching into the past: *My Father promised to take me to see The Boxing Kangaroos! But it was stripper joint—for a five-year-old! . . . My Mother would flop on her belly as she put it and turn the pages of a book as if just looking at the pages—no one believed she was reading but once I actually quizzed her—my own mother! . . . Do you remember the last time you were spanked— at Uncle Stanley's?* This last one is the only one where I've stopped him in his tracks, interjecting—*yes, and it isn't funny*—otherwise, I'd mumble, *yes, I think I've heard that one,* although he'd continue anyway. Now eighty-eight, his repeating such stories has gone on for decades as to become routine. Yesterday at a lunch, after his usual *Hi, how's that husband of yours!* and my continuing to pluck at my *chirashi-zushi,* I notice that as his short term memory shrinks, his distant memory has sharpened. And so his stories are increasingly new ones, so to speak, so now I say, *I've never heard of the one at your Grandparents' nightclub where your Grandpa used a knife to sweep the head off a beer!* When my husband visits him, Father suggests, *If she's bad, give her a spanking!* and my husband finally understands me.

LAURA KASISCHKE

Pathetic Fallacy

Secrets, hidden meanings, brief paths trampled through the grass, combed over again by the breeze on a summer day. (All the white doves turned to roses, and the white roses flew away.)

You truly believed you would escape from these? Like a moth with a wild cat's eyes painted on its wings, with no idea why the crows fly off in such a panicked racket each time you settle trembling on a branch?

Darwin, God, passing time, cryptic gifts and punishments. The way the fire turned to ashes seems to comment on desire. And the music, how it swelled perfectly with our suffering. And the rain began to fall as the wife described her husband's dying.

Some new, lost language on a virgin's tongue? Some garbled lullaby?

O, little sweet baby.
O, bittersweet lady.
O, illness & cradle & winter wheat fable.
O, sad gait of our injured neighbor.
O, ruined shoes of our maker, our translator.

MIRROR POEMS

So many poems have echoes and reflections in them, whether sonic or visual. When you look at these poems, you often see symmetry at some level. Mirror poems take reflection and recurrence and create something primordial, deeply intrinsic to the poem and its occasion. What happens in a mirror poem when you reflect something back on itself? You don't say something twice, but you create reflections and distortions similar to what you perceive in the mirror. Some mirroring poems have a perfect almost palindromic structure. Many mirror poems, though, create a fractured, distorted, or figurative image when things get reflected back on themselves. There is a relationship between interiority and reflection and, ironically, what is mirrored and reflected outwardly may often lead to a kind of inwardness.

Two mirror poems, published in *Poetry* magazine over several decades, served as the original inspiration for this section. Fred Chappell's echo poem, "Narcissus and Echo," is divided into two columns where the single word in the second column echoes the final word in the first column. In Randall Mann's poem, "Order," the first and last line, the second and penultimate line, etc., mirror each other. You will find examples of these mirroring structures in this anthology as well, along with a poem where words are mirrored within lines and a short poem which employs the mirroring of end-word homonyms.

QURAYSH ALI LANSANA
echolalia one

language echoing itself.
itself, echoing language
echoing language itself.
language, itself echoing

what i heard them say
say what? them, i heard.
heard them. what i say?
i say what them heard.

i mean these words
these words i mean.
mean these *i* words.
words mean: these, i.

why don't you hear me?
me you don't hear. why?
hear me, why don't you?
you don't? why? hear me.

you make me angry
angry you make me
make me angry: you
you angry. make me.

in my head i'm not alone.
alone, i'm not in my head.
head, i'm not in my alone
i'm in my head. not alone.

OLIVER BAEZ BENDORF

What Happens When We Die

Cardinal, who died and brought you here? I'm in bed,
driveway a ribbon of ice. Rattle from below.
States across the Midwest awoke to noise disturbance
jumping off the wall; in another, no discernable location.
When he was dying. I still think of him now, flapping—
unencumbered by the body? Stopping to see us all.

Sun lifts itself through gray over lake.
Morning my grandfather died, all of us—scattered—
in one case, curtains; in another, some knick-knack
all circa 4 a.m. Learned later
at the speed of—what—light? Energy,
on his way out of town.

On his way out of town
at the speed of—what—light? Energy,
all circa 4 a.m. Later learned
in one case, curtains; in another, some knick-knack
morning my grandfather died. We scattered
suns through gray over lake,

unencumbered by the body. Stopping to see us all
when he was dying. I still think of us now, flapping—
jumping off the wall; in another, no discernable location.
States across the Midwest awoke to noise disturbance,
driveway a ribbon of ice. Rattle from below. Cardinal
who died and brought you here to my bed.

KIMBERLY GREY

An Action

Mother is one. And I have, on occasion, been   *When*
painting, all winter long, watercolor bruises. My   *I*
god, I couldn't write, so I thought it was civilized to sink   *think*
them into paper: an accomplishment, thereof,   *of*
translating pain into color. I would have preferred   *her*
a brush, not *a thing done*: mother who left me needing   *reading*
the internet for tips on how to live motherless.   *This*
disobedience was civilized. I let the water ride,   *I*
let the blue run, a behavior of illustration linked   *think*
back to the Renaissance, a history of motherlove: *of*
art depicting the sublime: the act of choosing (not)   *bruising*
your child. Though I was never hit, I am quite sure,   *her*
acts of not-loving made of me an uncivilized design   *mind.*

SUZANNAH SPAAR

Thread a Pin Through Every Door, Drop the Line

Promise to moore   0   I promise to more

to tell you more soon   0   there's so much more

more house to see   0   more house to seed

after we nest   0   I nest.

Remember the birds
who build their homes   0
from scraps of tissue?

On snowy days the house   0   the unhoused snow,

was old. Drain rusted, so   0   old, I was drained was rusted so

I made a map too good   0   mapped for good

homes. Then I rested   0   Homes for resting.

Draw a map for me   You are no doubt

without doubt.   0   a map of me.

I am alive   0   I was alive then

But Florida sucks   0   But Florida sunk

and the sink clogged   0   and I sank, clogged

with his scraps   0   with his scraps

I met a very nice man	()	I met a man
he said, I can take you anywhere you need	()	he said, I can take you
but I just wanted to go	()	but I wanted to go
explore alone	()	alone
	()	No, I did not want to be alone.
I wanted to explore	()	
all of his old homes,	()	all of the homes I lived in
I called you from the road	()	I asked if you recalled
	()	the address.
The intimacy of a house besieged with winter.	()	When you flew to California It was with a soldered heart.
If I say	()	When I say
I miss you	()	I am remembering you
Remember	()	Miss
when we fried tomatoes	()	we fried red as tomatoes
in coconut oil	()	

                                      0   We were soldered in whiskey

the way you know to help   0   the way you know.

I don't know what to write   0   I wrote about

a man in fiction   0   a fiction

and a place and you   0   you were placed there too

Remember?   0

We were in love with men   0   we were in love

We ate tomatoes
from the pan,
                                      0
hearts halved
in hot oil.

What is more beautiful   0

than a road?   0   My friend,

I want your hand more   0   than I want my hand.

I love the desert   0   I love the desert

I will never leave   0   then leave.

Then onto what   0   toward what

do doors open?   0   Do they open

For the world of men or   0   for the world of solitude?

When the love-chase
across the fields is over   0
birds build their nests

I fly home   0   I fly to see you

and slam down the shade   0   and dawn is shaded

at take-off. A respite.   0   The sun is fervent.

    0   Who should have to bear such light?

TRACI BRIMHALL

Come, Slumberless

If blood sings from the ground, its song floods
the bones of prodigals. Paradise is for homebodies.
The rest of us bear the mark of our wandering.
In the amethyst hour I tape down my breasts.
On stage in my doublet, my love asleep. Banish
second chances, let me stay in the hour of radiant
dust and a prince's doom, dancing to the soundtrack
of God spinning zeros on the record table, a scratched
black night of bloodied milk and an art that prepares
itself for accidents. The ticks in the trees drop
at the smell of children. Jesus swings from the bells.
My bible the color of a scab and all my lines in red.
The merciless lullaby sings sin-bitten, hungering
like the heaven it doesn't resemble,
like the hell it does.

               Like hell it doesn't
marry the hungry to the sinners. The lullaby's mercy
ends like Jesus—faster than a thief, but still forever.
All his scabs redden like parables, and the small fears
swell like a tick in a child's ear. Art, like blood in
the milk. Record, like black in the silk. God dances
to a soundtrack of scratched zeroes. Prince by birth,
a king by death. On stage, I double. I banish sleep,
embrace my second chance. Mark my wandering,
how I bear it. A body is a home is a prodigal's
paradise. In the trysting hour I tape down my breasts,
call blood to answer the flood singing in the field.

JANUARY GILL O'NEIL

Bloom

An orchid grows inside of me,
blooms from a tight bud
in my chest, its milk-white petals
lean against the wall of my ribs.
Lost breaths, red heart bulging,
steady pulse of my soul shifting
in this incomplete landscape
of light. Loneliness takes root
with a beauty that surprises me,
suggests a kind of comfort,
feeds on everything I am.

*

It feeds on everything I am,
suggests a kind of comfort,
with a beauty that surprises me.
Loneliness takes root and light
in this incomplete landscape.
My soul shifts, steady pulse,
red heart bulging, lost breaths
lean against the wall of my ribs.
In my chest, milk-white petals
bloom from a tight bud,
an orchid grows inside of me.

HELEN SPICA

The Birch Swamp

Here,
silence is a bell and a loose clapper.

When I cried you said,
you can't see the forest for the trees;
a saying for the full head of summer,

birds above
hurling sound like the weather.

We move, after all, in the same direction,
like ash on the breath of fishermen,

each tree a joint—the machine presumed dead until eruption.

Like ash on the breath of fishermen
we move, after all, in the same direction,

hurling sound like the weather,
birds above.

A saying for the full head of summer:
You can see the forest for the trees.
As I cried you said,

silence is a bell and a loose clapper,
here.

MARILYN NELSON

Seventy

Suddenly I woke in the midst of life,
awake suddenly to the misseds of life
who disappeared into the mists of life.

ALEXANDRA TEAGUE

Studio with Blackened Windows

after Richard Diebenkorn

In Champaign-Urbana, Diebenkorn could not see.
Starkness left nothing for the mind to cling
to, burr on the coastal trail that it is. Burrower. Borrower. No
second room of light opened beyond his model's sleep-
dark head: a mirror tilting back her dreams
in the form of her hair, pillowed on her pillow. How far
into ourselves can we see? To know this, Diebenkorn knew,
we must start outside: ocean street-slant, palm tree, stop sign
stopping the eye like a red-winged blackbird in air that doesn't
stop. Matisse said: windows and walls don't divide; they extend
one space into another. Paint the room itself—
inside, outside—like a single country.
But how can anyone begin to imagine the heart of this country
if the heart of this country refuses to imagine itself?
It hurt to see. In self-preservation, he painted the glass—extending
night from his windows until the model's dark hair did
its best to copy zodiacs of birds and beasts and signs
of some familiar world continuing. Each day he knew
less. Where was the light the canvas needed: blankness stretched so far
it remembered its sailboats, streetlights blurred as dreams
in a desert rainstorm, the shadows of strangers? His paint slept
in Illinois. The country around him slept like a cupboard, no
food on the shelves, but a sign that read *Plenty* still clinging.
In the middle of America, Diebenkorn could not see.

VALERIE WALLACE

The Last Gardener of Aleppo

We ordinary people own the world
The bombs are Beethoven to us

The last gardener of Aleppo has been killed by a bomb
His son's eyes are bright coins

He stumbles from home to the white cemetery & does not see
The roundabouts citizens have planted, layers of green shrubs.

Rosemary, cedar, thyme, olive trees with no fruit;
How long they can tremble

No longer the question.
The father of flowers is gone & the garden is closed

To realize the world is ours before we leave it
What is that blessing?

Who will we sit with at the end, holding a tarnished spoon
How tender the leaves we twirl that fall in our glass cup

To own our world by holding in our chest the dark ka-booms
Of destruction & decide it is music

In the white morning, do we open the gates
Do we open the gates for morning

Do we open the gates for morning
In the white morning, do we open the gates

Of destruction & decide it is music
To own our world by holding in our chest the dark ka-booms

How tender the leaves we twirl that fall in our glass cup
Who will we sit with at the end, holding a tarnished spoon

What is that blessing?
To realize the world is ours before we leave it

The father of flowers is gone & the garden closed;
No longer the question

How long they can tremble.
Rosemary, cedar, thyme, olive trees with no fruit;

The roundabouts citizens have planted, layers of green shrubs.
He stumbles from home to the white cemetery

His son's eyes are bright coins
The last gardener of Aleppo has been killed by a bomb

The bombs are Beethoven to us
We ordinary people own the world

CONCRETE POEMS

A concrete (or shaped) poem combines form and subject, resulting in a work that visually resembles or invokes its topic. Generally, this adds a degree of playfulness in the composition and reading of the poem. A poet writing a concrete poem, as with any form, must decide how to shape a poem so that the form is integrated into the subject matter, instead of perched on top of it; in the best concrete poems, shape is not merely decorative—it is essential to the poem. The concrete poem becomes something pictorial and offers a hybrid version of the poem as art.

George Herbert's "Easter Wings" is a well-known example of striking shaped poetry.

ELEANOR WILNER

Before Our Eyes

the one who has fallen:
bird with beak wide open.
dog rigid on the kitchen floor,
naked fledgling on the sidewalk
below the useless nest. Or the star-
fish left by the tide's withdrawal, still
breathing through its tubal arms but not
for long; even so, the slug making its slow
way across the paving in a drought will never
reach the damp for which, in sluggish thoughts, it
lusts. And woe to the sloth who moves so syrupy slow,
who can't escape the fast approaching walls of roaring fire.
All the fallen, and then the million leaves, and it is fall, and we
are sore afraid. For now the falling has come to our block, to our
neighborhood; the sound of splintering wood, the thunder of falling
bricks is everywhere. Nowhere to hide, even the longest line must reach
the limits of the page, and age take its toll, and what was sure, must fail, and fall.

But then, as when a ball of yarn is wound up from the long unravel of a failed
attempt to knit, the pattern lost, the knitter on to other things, or when
the great thread in the hero's hand be slowly gathered in, and he
return through the high walls of the maze to the sunlit mouth,
or the leaves of autumn be raked and piled, and set to burn,
the ashes at rest in the urn, or the small boat unwind
the rope and lift the anchor to the stern, the boat
raise its small sail, the sailor holding the line
that sets the sheet to the wind, the tiller
firm in her hand, the wind rising,
the little craft heading into
the rising sun, the sheen
on the sea a shield
against the dark;
even a dinghy
can be an
ark, day
in, day
out.

PHILLIP COZZI

Hong Kong Crane

After H.W. Leung

How
privileged
to have known
you, if only briefly,
skyping from your
island home. Not
bad privilege
of which
I am both
accused and
guilty. But
the good kind,
that of having
been a lodger
in my mother,
from comma
to paragraph,
of positing
paired femurs,
chambers of
the heart, to
be vertebrate,
mammal and
mortal, and if
one day, our poet-farmer,
your gaze lifts from swampy gallery
to find a crane, beak-tipped, across a shallow
pond as if standing in portrait, may your artist's
soul migrate toward a view with two focal points,
us and them, sketch a horizontal line, trace words
of grass to occupy the foreground, light washing
water, and tranquility alight as in a moment
of acceptance of guilt. The perspective of
sky to land is as significant as the sense
of scale: a view from a cluster of
cells clinging to endometrium,
the gender   of a poem,
the   flight
of   text,
                  the
                  b
                  a
                  l
                  a
                  n
                  c
                  e
of colors compressed toward horizon, the rare privilege that is ours.

VICTORIA CHANG

Obit

Language—died, brilliant and beautiful
on August 1, 2009 at 2:46 pm. Letters
used to skim my father's brain before
they let go. Now his words are blind.
Are pleated. Are the dispatcher, the
dispatches, and the receiver. When my
mother was dying, I made everyone
stand around the bed for what would
be the last group photo. Some of us
even smiled. Because dying lasts forever
until it stops. Someone said, *take a few*.
Someone said, *say cheese*. Someone said,
thank you. My mother couldn't speak
but her eyes were the only ones that were
wide open. Language fails us. In the way
that *breaking an arm* means an arm's
bone can break but that the arm itself
can't break off unless sawed or cut.

CHRIS GREEN

Apollinaire's Ex-Girlfriends in the Snow

after "It's Raining," Guillaume Apollinaire

There   days   in

            are   January

          when

                the sky

                          is

                                filled

with Maries

            and   Madeleines

        ex

                muses all

    their

            clothes

                are   heavy

      their

            music

                        slow

  a   dusting

              of

                  ghosts

  a

        lowering

and
the man   walking   away

ROBIN REAGLER

Skyscraper

Up to a certain
point we all agree,
boys will be boys.
A skyscraper is his
way of saying, we can
make mountains too.
And so this emblem
of human arrogance
towers, a flamboyant
speaking spectacle
of achievement.
Consider phallic
Monadnock, a New
England hill relocated
to old Chicago. Or
the Chrysler Building
mounted by Margaret
Bourke-White shooting
photos of steely gargoyles
or Annie Leibovitz years later.
Nature has its laws;
and we have our desire,
standing up straight,
gleaming like godhead,
reminding us how
instantly the future flashes.

ELLEN RACHLIN AND GEORGIY ZHIKHAREV

A Brief History of Writing

Sharp reeds marched
early thoughts into clay where
doubt's arrows and logic's wedges
scarcely survived in cuneiform rooms.
Flat leaves and stems bore wounds
with salves of ink birds—
spontaneity revealed much too
late. Evolved, into molted
feather we tucked ink—lent
ideas the gift of flight, easing
minds of their weight, yet
strong enough to bear the
perfect and the mistake
as joining barb to slash
of vane. With quill
what was crossed
through, we could retrace
where we lost our place,
and second guess if wrong
was right and pathway out.
Then graphite's ease
edged feather out,
fraying ties to
nature's
flight. And
soon
there-
after the
space for
im
per
fec
ti
on's
h
i
s
tory wiped clean by a simple, square plastic   **backspace**

RAVI SHANKAR

A Is for Arbor

Fret-
work red
cedar bones
exposed before
vines twine tendrils
in privacy and shade
that keeps the neighbors
from surveying too closely the very idea
of family they enact when no one is there to
set the record straight, no one
to see them set each other off
like car alarms or black powder
fireworks in some Chinatown
celebrating the Year of the Rat

COLLAGE POEMS

The collage poem, borrowing a practice from the visual arts, enables poets to appropriate work from other sources. The word, collage, derives from the French, "a pasting" or from the Old French, *coller, "to glue."* In collaging, you lift from other sources and attempt to integrate the borrowed texts within your own original lines. There is a sense of movie editing in writing a collage poem, where you employ cinematic techniques of a montage sequence such as cross-cutting, dissolving, fading and splicing.

A collage poem is an announcement that you are incorporating things from others you read or hear. You might write down favorite lines by other authors or else record snippets of conversation to incorporate into your own work, transplanting and teasing things together. The beauty of creating a collage poem is to take foreign sources and arrange them in dialogue with each other. What is the frisson—the yoking of disparate elements, the quickfire juxtapositions—that can be accomplished? Poets also use the collage technique as a way to create tension down the page, braiding or interweaving different strands of narratives.

There are various types of collage poems, most notably, the cento where every line is taken from someone else. In a found poem, you discover something "unpoetic" in life such as an excerpt from a newspaper or a map and translate the primary document into a poem. Erasure poems take a primary text and then, by deleting lines, create a new poem. All these types of collage poems suggest a direct engagement with some other text where you establish an engagement with the source text. The process of the poem is inherent in the collage poem as you witness the mind at work.

DAVID BAKER

Checkpoint

These are the days when birds come back.

These are the days the birds. These days

these birds. These days are these birds.

Let us see these days these papers. When

are these birds, and where are your papers.

Where are you going. Come back answer

me where you are going. Behind the barn,

the flame tree, our fire, our wings, these birds,

behind the trees the bursting winds the birds.

These days come back. They do not, there

what color is your ruby-throat, your toothbrush

yellow-breasted warbler green flame blue-

jay marsh thrush among the light the lush, low

timid leaf she said by the river what fire

is your nova is your wife's hairbrush

take off your shoes take your hands off

stop right there so many coming over as

so many millions fewer wings these papers

of fragile bones vanished they are not

where are you going I said come back.

Things I Am Beginning to Forget

after Pillow Book, *Sei Shonagon*

I cannot recall who exactly was told what by whom when my mother died. I know that Ted jumped from our bed to answer the phone at—what? was it 1 am? My parents' neighbor Mrs. Sugg called to tell us. But then, did I answer the detective's call that night or the next day—? I do remember that I pulled on a pair of trousers that were slightly formal instead of jeans—it seemed more appropriate wear for the visit to the E.R. to see my father who did not yet know that mother was dead. That she had died "instantly." I do remember that Ted called Doug to get a cab uptown to take care of our girls. And that I called my sister but only told her that there had been an accident—or did I tell her mother was dead?

Date of last period: _____
Date of last mammogram: _____

[e-mail to PZ] *My dates in college? I know I didn't go out with Tony but maybe Dana? Was hanging out in a bedroom dating in 1973? And who cares? I do know that parents back then would think so and care and say so. In fact, I'd never admit to my parents, especially my father, that any guy had entered my dorm room (were you in Hillcrest?). Who asks for such grief which is mostly what I tend to remember. And you? Didn't you go out with a guy who ended up making hamburger commercials? And what about that guy who starved himself before going for an Army physical—was that your roommate's boyfriend or mine?*

Now, what did I walk into this room for . . .

I immediately forget the plots of novels and now I forget if I've even read, say, *Widow Basquiat*—though I must have, given how much I love Jennifer's writing.

You cannot make Remembrance grow
When it has lost its Root—
[?]
At a Window facing West—[is that the next line—? and then?]

Olive oil?

SIMONE MUENCH

Wolf Cento

(all lines and fragments from Larry Levis)

Compose the dark, compose
a list of what I cannot touch:

stone, song, trembling, waist, & snow,
the boy who wished to stay awake forever.

I don't see anything at the end of it
except an endlessness—

one endless, empty window
on what had to be. Nothing more

than a light summer dress
when the body has gone

too quiet to hear
& smells its way to the sea.

& what do you do
when nothing calls you anymore?—

The suicides slip beneath you, shining.
The soul rests its head in its hands & stares out

at the sun taking its place again
all through the empty summer—

as empty as the skull of an owl, a wolf
thin with disease—something beyond

all recognition; a music stripped
of all prayer. From now, I will wake

to the gleaming of frost on someone's lawn.
The morning will be bright, & wrong.

The Cloistered Life of Nuns

In Reading Market, you recall a fisherman in Sifnos
fetch a snapper sloshing in a tub, the quick motions
of snipping needlepoint fins and, tail to head,
rake with the backside of a fillet knife
so that little translucent scales seem to burst
like a frenzy of designs from the Age of Enlightenment.

The mind sweeps empty opening into night.

A poacher hacks the face of an elephant and
tugs at ivory tusk as the driver listens
to Ragamuffin while reading Job 40:15.

Suppose there is an Architect or a Gnostic,
what consciousness could we ever possess?
The Discontents rioted today. On spatial scale,
Plato held the ideal Republic should glimmer into sight.

A German shepherd barks at a rabbit secreted in a hedgerow
over genial chatter at a summer party as water striders
dogpaddle on a manmade pond in sync. The carnage

was a way of life like a plain gold ring inscribed
with a single word: Love.

You touched a peach and saw in your mind the cloistered life
of nuns descending stairwells like moths. So much crushed ice,
spilling on the floor out of the crates, stilled fish eyes marbling.

Behold now behemoth, which I made with thee; he eateth grass as an ox.

ELIZABETH BRADFIELD

Lesson III: The Divisions, Illustrated

redacted from page 9 of Smith's Quarto, *or* Second Book in Geography, *1848*

What are Oceans?   Ocean? (see the corners of
the Maps.) What ocean separates   ? America
from Africa? America from Asia?

    Name the oceans?

A SEA is a large body.   The whole body
    sometimes.

        Africa from Europe?
Africa from Asia?   southeast of Asia?   East of
    What sea?   Ocean?   Which?

      sea, interspersed

A GULF   a body
    extending.

What gulf ?
    What?

A STRAIT is a narrow body.
      America? separate   connect
    straits   What, between?
What do they connect?

    connected and   separated   each

A LAKE is a body. The water &c., is
    The water.
How long?

        water flowing
  into an   other body.

Into what does it flow?   Into what does it
flow?
               Into what do they unitedly flow?
         Into what do they flow?
     Africa, into what does it flow?
Asia, and into what do they flow?
     natural divisions   ?

Name the Grand Divisions.
    largest   ?   Largest ?
Largest?   Largest   ? Largest gulf?

MARTHA COLLINS

We Listen We Pray

Advent 2017

In those   days   after   that the

agencies   system   deportation

sun   shall be   darkened and

police   weapons   refugees

the moon   shall not   give her

hurricanes   earthquakes   wars

the stars   of heaven   shall fall

*

rend   the heavens   mountains

workers without   nuclear   world

flow   down fire   waters   to boil

Palestine   Israel   Yemen   Iraq

nations   presence   tremble before

desperate   facing   awake

a leaf   the wind   clay

*

to bind up   the broken   to open

transitions   to say   all   the living

ashes   oil   joy   for mourning

peace   increase   change of   courage

planting   the garden   earth our

prayers   are requested for

not   the light   but the voice

ELIZABETH SPIRES

Found Poem: The Couple Who Lived at the Mall

assembled from articles by Lisa Selin Davis on Salon *and in* The Week

A mall: four floors, 170 shops, and eight restaurants.
It was going up on thirteen prime acres,
and old Kingsley Avenue was now glittering Providence Place
so Michael and Adriana, a smart young couple,
part of an art collective, decided, in protest, to live there.
Theirs was a critique. An embrace. A performance piece.
They found an empty storage space, crafted a secret
apartment, moved in with flashlights and space blankets,
planning to stay a week.

But even a week involved camouflage:
they carried empty Nordstrom shopping bags,
wore khakis and button-down shirts.

"We're all asked to be performance artists," Adriana said.
"We're all being watched."

After four days, they felt euphoric, "bored yet ecstatic."
"It was better for me than any nature walk
I've ever taken," said Michael, "but it only works
if you don't bring any money or your cell phone."
A week stretched into months, then a year, four years.
They brought in sofas, tables, lamps, a TV, a play station.
They had plans to install wood floors and a portable toilet.

They believed in the future, imagined having a child.
"We wanted our child to have its birthday there.
We wanted the baby's first steps to be in the mall."

It might have gone on forever,
but they posted their whereabouts on the Web.
Expelled by the management, they had their two minutes
of fame on *The Early Show.*

General Growth Properties, the mall's owner,
feels "violated" and has returned their furniture.
And their wedding video, taken
paddling past the mall on the Woonesquaktucket River.

KEVIN PRUFER

Hog Kaput

Because we couldn't control their population
and because they destroyed our parks
and farmlands,
                    we proposed
to place in troughs a kind of poison
called Hog Kaput.
                         The poison, a blood thinner, killed
humanely,
                  and in the video we presented to the legislature,
the hog in the lab took only a few steps
before falling on its side.

*

                    Hello,
said the feeding trough to the hungry hog.
Come here.
                At first, the hog eyed the metal trough
with suspicion. He'd grown accustomed
to the pleasures of the farmer's field
                         and that place
by the riverbank where the wild blackberry brambles
tickled his hide.
                How the sunlight dappled
the muddy water and warmed his thick neck. *C'mon,*
said the trough, and the hog
                      lumbered over,
lifted the lid with his snout, sniffed the pellets,
pushed his face inside.

*

                  Heavy as shit, said the workman
after he'd removed the dead hog from the testing room,
hosed the floor clean,
                  and washed his hands.

Heavy as shit, he told the pregnant young woman
he'd married one year before, exactly,

                    who sat across from him
while the waiter set two bowls of soup gracefully
on the table,
          gotta feel bad for the poor fucker,
he said,
        and she smiled because, yes, his wasn't an easy job,
but somebody, she told herself, somebody
                    had to do it.

*

By any definition,
              they were an invasive species,
and the citizen farmers asked only
that their lands not be disturbed.
                 Shooting them
from helicopters
           accomplished little—there were just
too many—
          and even if we unintentionally
poisoned scavengers that fed on their meat,
it was a small price to pay
to keep our American parks
                untrammelled,
and to satisfy our farmers—

*

You see,
he told his pregnant wife,
            the trouble is they reproduce, so two of them
become a thousand,
         and pretty soon it's hogs everywhere,
hogs like you wouldn't believe,

roving gangs of hogs,
and she blew gently on the spoonful of soup,
sipped it,
            then looked up, smiling.

*

It tasted of carrot, it tasted
of wild potato, burdock root and turnip, parsnip
and sunchoke,
            and the hog ate and ate from the trough,
until he had his fill.
            Then the lid snapped shut,
and he took a step toward the river,
                        where the others
lay on the banks in sunlight,
            and from the corners of his eyes,
a delightful sparkling,
            a kind of flicker, a thousand
fireflies crowding his vision,
            beautiful, really,
and he took another step
            into what was now
a kind of snow storm—

*

            So we can have meat for the table,
so we can protect the fields,
            because some species are
invasive,
      because our country needs protection,
because we inhabit the land
the way an ideal
            inhabits the mind—
we submitted our proposal to the legislature,

hoping they would understand why it was vital that,
at all costs,

           we saw to the elimination of the hogs.

*

Yes, he said, it had been a very good meal,
a nice anniversary,

              his wife was happy, yes, she was,
he could tell because,

                 when he helped her into the car,
then leaned inside to hand her the Styrofoam box
filled with leftovers,

             she reached out to him,
surprised him,

           kissing him suddenly on the mouth,
and squeezing his hand.

              So now, driving home
past the woods, now empty of hogs,
with her beside him—

             the three of them, really,
if you counted the baby—

               well, who could be happier
than he was?

STATEMENTS ABOUT THE POEMS
BY THE POETS

ARS POETICA

"Break My Heart," Joy Harjo

You will not find much prose from me regarding the craft of poetry, or regarding any kind of deconstruction of the why and how of poetry. Of course, there is an art, even science if you will to the writing of a poem. There's architecture, there are aesthetics, and attention to orality. There are poetry ancestors from which every poem is descended. There is a country, land, and a generation from which the poet emerges with poems in hand and heart. I would never have written poetry if the nomenclature and rules for making poetry were impressed on me before I experienced the magic of reading, listening to, and hearing poetry. Poetry emerges from the land of no words, into a house, houses, whole countries of words. Everyone has their own way of approaching the craft. For me each poem is a journey through a crack in a broken heart. I hear a voice, a rhythm or a melody and I follow. I attempt to leave a path behind me of the most intriguing lines of sound and meaning, something I could never imagine, until now.

"Delivery," Martha Rhodes

I don't set out to write a poem, let alone a poem about . . .

There is this drifting that happens—and then I end up . . . somewhere, and that's what I care about as a writer—moving myself and my reader across and down the page, and *into*. Aristotle sat me down one day, as he was writing his *Poetics*, and told me (I paraphrase here) that the poet's work is not to chronicle that which happens but to bring to page that which may have happened, may be so. We spoke early on in my writing "career." I went along with him then, and do now—I don't set out to report, or to be a spokesperson, or teller of anything. That I am even *I* in the poem, or you are *you*—matters not. What matters is that I *may* be I, you *may* be you. That *may* be so. One syllable attaches to space or to another syllable and the music that's created—well, that music is what drives me home, brings me to what may be so on the page—the syllables attaching to each other and to the space surrounding brings me driftingly through, encouraging me to go along, push against—and ideally (Frost, here), *you*('ll) *come too.*

"The Uses of What Is Hollow," Eleanor Wilner

How to write poetry in this hollow time in America? The Greek myth of Pan and Syrinx returned to memory: how Pan, the lusty nature god, pursued the chaste nymph Syrinx; how the river nymphs answered her cry by turning her into a bed of reeds; and how Pan turned the reeds into the plaintive music of the panpipe (also called syrinx). Then the poem wrote itself. In the high Andes, the panpipes flourish, and the most haunting of those Peruvian songs is *el condor pasa*, finding musical form for the flight of the condor, vulture through whom dead matter is transformed into living flesh, as breath transforms hollow absence into song.

"Ars Poetica," Mai Der Vang

In reflecting on the craft and artistry of writing poetry, I'm keen to remind myself that poetry is not always about finding answers. Often, a poem can lead to more questions that moves it beyond the possibility of any rational outcome. But a poem can also lead to surprising discoveries in language, form, or imagery, which in some ways can be viewed as the answers themselves. Perhaps that's why in this poem, there are moments where the logic feels very elusive and jarring yet the language and imagery seem to leap forward in an attempt to flip themselves inside out. I also try to explore my own literary history, or lack thereof. Coming from a primarily oral culture that did not have a definitive writing system until recently, as a writer, I struggled to make sense of the spoken and written worlds as gestured to in the fourth stanza. That unlettered part of who I am is ingrained into the ways I approach the craft of writing.

"The Lights Burn Blue," Alan Michael Parker

There was of course a bird outside my studio window—the simplest of fleeting pleasures—and then a second bird disagreed with the rights of the first. I felt like a judge, no Solomon but inspired nonetheless to say which of the birds was blue. The poet-speaker in the poem—thinking through color, and how to describe in words the different colors of the two birds—is led to consider the writing of poems, and his/her own obsession with the limits of language. All of the ensuing sonic play in the poem matters greatly, as the poet-speaker considers too how sounds make meaning. That the poet-speaker laughs at his earlier self, or at least lightly scolds, seems to me consistent with an *Ars Poetica*; I trust more deeply aesthetics that change over time, rather than claim eternal currency. Notwithstanding, when it comes to the color "blue" and the writing of a poem, to name remains the goal: I am hoping the poem names a scene, a phenomenon, and an idea, and thereby once more affirms the poet-speaker's existence. I like believing I exist: poems help me do this.

"Mother (of Poetry)," Allison Seay

I have been writing a series of poems that work with a contoured equation aligning motherhood with the art of poetry. As I write this, I am eight months pregnant with my first child and living in an awe-inspired fog. It has been a long season of waiting; ideas about birth, creation, origin, what it means to *make something*—and make meaning *of* something—have blurred, complicated, and inspired the metaphors of pregnancy; the literal and figurative "conception," "gestation," "birth" of human beings and of poetry feels like incredibly rich territory to explore. (No wonder there is, universally, so much in art, literature, and song that seeks to make sense of it all.) A divine coincidence: motherhood and poetry. Of course, I think that we all—even those who are not women, or mothers, or mothers-to-be—are all living with this fertile possibility all the time. We're *all* embodiments of *ars poetica,* existing as both muse and maker, the very metaphor we seek to describe. I intended this poem, "Mother (of Poetry)," to be a meditation on what it means to be something made from nothing: we weren't, and then we were. And we continue being.

"The Invention of the F-hole," Kimberly Johnson

A couple of years ago, I read an article by some MIT mechanical engineers about the optimal sonic properties of the *f*-shaped holes in violins. In the early days of luthiery, the violin's ancestor instrument had circular holes, which over time evolved into half-moons, and thence into C-shaped holes in a variety of elaborations, until finally the Amati masters of 16th-century Cremona, Italy, contrived the sound hole in the distinctive shape of today's violins. This poem developed out of that article, and out of my subsequent musings about the relationship between form and function, especially as it relates to poetry. Poetry offers a highly constructed form of utterance, ostentatious in its embellishments and artifices even when it doesn't employ traditional form. Certainly, there are rational justifications for form (memorability, the forging of associations between ideas through parallel structures and features like rhyme, etc.) but surely pleasure—incalculable as it is—must be one motivation. Surely beauty. We long to hold moving things, to keep and care for them. Things like air and sound and love and life. This poem considers *form*—in wood, in words—as one expression of that careful urge to keep.

"Ars Poetica," Cornelius Eady

Is poetry about the work or about the recognition of the work? This poem arose, I believe, from an exercise I gave my students in a poetry class that I taught at the University of Missouri. I wrote with them, and it tossed me back to a Halloween, years ago, in my hometown of Rochester, NY. My parents' house sat on a corner lot, and across the street, an aunt owned a small, almost cottage-like house, where she lived with her husband, and no kids.

What did they do for a living? Why didn't they have any children, and why did they never, ever cross the street to visit? These are questions I can't answer, even to this day. Writing there, in class, I thought of myself, a kid, caught in the light of my aunt's open door, waiting for her to call me family, and never hearing it. They are all gone, now. Both the houses are still standing, however, and if I went back to that block, I know, just as they are a story with chapters I can never fill in, that I am a tale they'll never know the ending to.

LITANIES, CATALOGS, & LISTS

"For Our People," Angela Jackson

Having shown honor to DuBois and Hayden, I decided to show equal respect to a poet with whom I had a personal relationship. Margaret Walker was my African-American Literature Professor at Northwestern University. I remember how she stood at the front of the large lecture room and recited her masterpiece "For My People" written in 1942. It is still powerful today. And her kindness and encouragement remain with me. I knew I had to pay homage to her and her magnificent poem of a people. I poured myself into my new century poem, "For Our People." "For My People" is known for its cascading rhythm, its Biblical, hypnotic chant quality. It is a litany of details of Black life. I would do the same in "For Our People." I struggled with the title because I know my people are bigger than me, more diverse than Walker's. I would be as an African priest performing a ritual of respect for Black people and searching out the words to create a future. I believe in *nommo*, a Bantu word for word-magic, the evocative power of the word to make material change. So it is with "For Our People" and the force of Love itself.

A litany uses repetition of key phrase or phrases to create its powerful, mesmerizing effect. I repeated the phrase "for our people," honing in on the multitudinous aspects of the people of which I speak and lifting up our experience and selves at the same time in this ritual litany. There is a pulse, a heartbeat in this litany and its details. According to critic Bob Thompson, one of the criteria of Yoruba art and sculpture is "repetition of changes." This is significant to "For Our People" as well, for the poem does not repeat monotonously but moves unexpectedly, piling on moments and incidents authentic and sensitive to the Black experience, gathering momentum until it reaches a crescendo. I worked for the ending, over and over. I began "For Our People" in 2012 or 2013 and completed it in 2017. I hope my teacher is pleased. I hope I have honored my esteemed ancestor with this litany.

"Political Poem," Joy Ladin

This poem grows out of my efforts to reckon with my own whiteness, with the ways being white has affected my life. I wrote it in response to my realization a year or two ago that the reason my family owned a lovely house despite having one lower-middle-class income was that our neighborhood was red-lined, reserved for white people. Suddenly I grasped how utterly being white had shaped my life. This poem is an effort to not only remember my childhood but to re-imagine it to include the whiteness I literally grew up inside, a whiteness that, in ways I still don't understand, colored my most intimate experiences, including my relationship with my mother. In it, that work of re-imagining, making visible the whiteness that was invisible to me, is done through the repetition: I insert the word "whiteness" into a list of elements of my childhood, and—this feels like the most dangerous aspect of the poem—forcibly couple it with the word "love." I still don't understand how whiteness shaped my love. As poets have done since the earliest prayers, I approach mystery through invocation, hoping the power of language will carry me beyond my understanding.

"From the Word *Go*," Anna Leahy

"From the Word *Go*" is formed by a list of idioms or phrases that have developed particular cultural meaning from repeated use. So, repetition is built into the idea of what an idiom is. Though there are many more *go* idioms that did not make it into this poem, the word *go* appears fifteen times and constitutes more than one-fifth of the poem's words. That repetition invites expectation—the reader knows another *go* is probably coming—and also invites variation across idioms as the poem moves forward through different phrases. Many of the idioms may sound familiar to the reader, though some are combined or shifted slightly. Combining common expressions emphasizes that the same word can be used to create mutually exclusive meanings, as *go into effect* and *go out of fashion,* for instance, are somewhat opposite concepts. The word *go* is a short verb that indicates movement, and it is used in this poem in the form of a command. Repeating the imperative form of this verb is a way to make the poem sound especially insistent, perhaps relentless. By using turns of phrase based on this word in this form, the poem explores a variety of pressures we face, things we are supposed to do or not do, and options we have or decisions we make as we move through life.

"descendent," Quraysh Ali Lansana

I wrote this poem for the 50th anniversary of AfriCOBRA (African Commune of Bad Relevant Artists), which was one of the most important and influential artist collectives of the Black Arts Movement of the 1960s and 1970s, and, in my opinion, among this country's most critical collectives of creative, political people. The italicized couplet is language from a painting by AfriCOBRA co-founder Barbara Jones-Hogu. The poem is an homage to Miss Jones-Hogu, her painting, and the never-ending need to speak truth to power. The use of anaphora and function in an effort to highlight the truth that little has changed regarding racial politics concerning Black Americans.

"Waiting for Greece's Fate on Serifos," Aliki Barnstone

A while back, a Facebook post went viral, asking people to list "10 Things You Don't Know about Me," and I wrote a poem with that title. The form intrigued me, and when the Greek economic and the refugee crises intensified, I found I could write only list poems.

These poems became my book-in-progress, *Happenstance*. So much of our life situation is happenstance. We don't choose our parents, genetics, ethnicity, or where we are born, just as refugees don't choose to flee war or to be driven from their homes because of their ethnicity or to lose their farms because of drought caused by climate change. List poems such as "Waiting for Greece's Fate on Serifos" attend to the confounding, seemingly disparate things that consciousness links together and strain against lyric even as they engage in it.

My mother is Greek. Summers, I live on the island of Serifos. In 2015, the banks closed, then capital controls were imposed. The economic foundation we took for granted was destabilized. As we obsessively checked our smart phones for the news, I remembered the days on Serifos when we couldn't count on water running from the taps. The list poem allows me to expand the lyric moment and connect whatever presents itself, whether it be a dream, an old fountain, the 24-hour news cycle, or social media—which started me on this journey.

"The Afterlife of American Poets," Billy Collins

At a reception after a poetry reading, I overheard someone remark, "Robert Frost would be spinning in his grave." That got me thinking about other ways to picture Frost in his current state. Maybe he was wandering in a yellow wood or how about resting on a log of gold? And what about all the others? I've written only one or two other list poems, but it's a pleasing form in that it invites reader participation. Readers play along because they know what will come next (here, another poet) without knowing exactly what (which poet plus the accompanying image). That state of mind (knowing / not knowing) is evoked by the meter and rhyme scheme of all formal poems, yet informal poems can convey a similar pleasure if the poet tips off the reader about the game that is now underway. The right title can do the trick, so can a card turned over early on. Plus, list poems are fun to write. Blanks appear and you fill them in.

"Litany," Christina Pugh

"Litany" was written at the beginning of a month-long stay in an Italian villa on the Ligurian Sea. The poem and its language formed a response not only to the considerable beauty of these surroundings but also to the incessant sound of the tides, from which one never gets a break (as it were). Just as a litany makes use of repeated words and sounds, so does the sea repeat itself non-verbally; I hoped to approximate that inexorability by incorporating a series of questions and internal rhymes into the poem. But the poem is not just mimetic of what the sea does. It also comprises a wish, or a prayer, to be "permeable" to the sea's sounds. It's not always clear how to create that permeability, or how a human subject might become less separate from the natural world. But one possible strategy is to voice one's own litany in dialogue with the watery litany one hears. In that particular sense, "Litany" is a poem that is hoping to learn the sea's language.

"Select an Answer," Oliver de la Paz

As parents of newly diagnosed children on the autism spectrum, my wife and I steeled ourselves against the outside world, fearing our children would be ostracized and even endangered because of their difference. Part of my process in writing my recent poems, as part of a manuscript entitled *The Boy in the Labyrinth*, is realizing the limits of my thinking and the expectations I had for raising a neurotypical child. The labyrinths I negotiate every day as Father to sons on the autism spectrum are the ways that language sometimes does not convey direct "if / then" causality. Words can disguise human intentions, a difficult lesson for someone who is on the autistic spectrum to comprehend. The template form of the "Select an Answer" type found in standardized tests provide a certitude of structure my children can understand—a way of limiting the options for them because in their specific case they can often get overwhelmed with all the possibilities that arise from any given social interaction. The hybridized form of the "Select an Answer" enabled me to address some of the personal concerns that I had originally felt in writing as a neurotypical parent about perspectives of a neurodiverse child, as well as reaching an understanding about the limits of my knowledge or the realm of my permission.

"Titles from Harold's Shelf, A Portrait," Kimiko Hahn

The spines in a person's library can be (should be?) very telling—to the extent that the owner's character is revealed. By most standards, my husband, Harold, is an extremely eclectic reader, wolfing down children's stories or a rock star's bio, or some aspect of 19th century furniture. But they all make perfect sense to one who knows him and his work. I hoped to use this eclectic list to reveal a specific character to his eccentricity. Is this poetry? In a list form, if the diction and imagery and tone are varied, there is an electricity that creates the heightened quality one looks for in art. And repetition (evil, chain saw, murder, Smutty) can create the kind of binding element that I expect in art. Deviation from repetition plays against expectation and offers progression: *where am I being led?* From punishment to faith to hunger. I hope that the overall feeling is a sense of the uncanny. (I hasten to note that all of these volumes are real except for *Celia Thaxter Selected Poems*. She never published a collection but Harold researched her poetry for his own work. I call this bit of fabrication *poetic license*.)

"Questions for Google," Elizabeth Spires

Ever since reading Phillis Levin's "Unsolicited Survey," a delicate, mysterious poem comprised completely of unanswered questions, I have wanted to write a poem in the interrogative mode. A series of questions, I've come to realize, can create or suggest a narrative, a state of mind or mood, a general atmosphere. And questions, through word choice, tone, and syntax, can conjure a distinct speaking voice and even point to who or what is listening (or not listening).

This got me to thinking about Google's ubiquitous presence in our lives, used everyday in search of basic, pedestrian *facts*: a street address, biographical information, timetables, etc. But what if Google could supply the answers to philosophical and metaphysical questions? What if Google knew the answers to *all* of our questions? Out of curiosity, I typed in, "What is the meaning of life?" As of yesterday, 649,000,000 results came up. Really.

Writing "Questions for Google" reinforced what I already knew: a question asked in a poem is almost always better left unanswered. Just go back and reread Yeats's late great poem "Among Schoolchildren," and you'll see what I mean.

"Things I Find in Abuela's Bathroom Closet," Rigoberto González

I'm currently obsessed with Sei Shōnagon's *The Pillow Book*, a record of her musings and observations during her time as a member of the emperor's court in 11th century Japan. Each of her lists is wondrous because it moves beyond description and creates a narrative, and I tried to tap into that potential with this poem about the things I found in my grandmother's bathroom closet. I wanted to examine how our possessions define us, reveal us, amuse us, and betray us. I wanted to explore how belongings outline our cultural identities, our sexualities, our desires, and our insecurities. In this case, I had some fun with the notion of secrets—the young boy's and his grandmother's—and how they intersect in such an intimate space, and how even in a place that demands discretion and privacy, there is room for expression and a bit of freedom.

EPISTLES & POSTCARDS

"Our Fault Is We Love Too Much," Ira Sukrungruang

For a time, I thought poetry had left me. But then I thought: *this is foolish.* Poetry never leaves; rather, you leave poetry. So I left for a bit. I left because I entered an internal spiral, the "darkness" that Styron wrote about in *Darkness*

Visible. I turned to Richard Hugo's *31 Letters and 13 Dreams.* I still remember where I read that book—on an enormous bean bag that swallowed me. Hugo's poems, moreover his letter poems, swallowed me. There he wrote about his own struggles, relaying vulnerability to some of his closest friends—Charles Simic, Marvin Bell, Carolyn Kizer. His letters reminded me that I need not isolate myself from the world. That poetry was a way of connecting, of reaching out. This letter poem to a close friend was my first poem in years, was a poem that "somewhat" admitted my state in life to another. This poem was a way to say something but not say something. But that is the beauty of a letter. Sometimes its purpose is to announce you are there.

"With Love from Ainezalandia," Elizabeth Macklin

This scene was probably my very first entry into Ainezalandia, an invented country that is the subject of a long reportage poem called *With Love from Ainezalandia.* The actual market was directly across the river from the apartment I rented in Bilbao during my Amy Lowell Poetry Travelling Scholarship year, which I spent in Spain's Basque Country. The gulls did come on the dot of the hour, every day. Later, the city's renovation of the market changed the colors, but even so it looks like a ferryboat; when it was built it was said to be the largest municipal market in Europe. It turned out that in Basque grammar there was a way to express what the gulls were doing.

"Dear Art," Cynthia Atkins

There is something about the act of letter writing that is wholly unique. It is a genre that holds both private commentary and historical cues—a portal used to express love, philosophy, religion, and morality (not to mention the private thoughts of one entity to another). There is almost nothing more intimate, exacting, and even romantic. The notion of distance, geographical and otherwise is part of this perspective. Our earliest origins expose these missives on cave walls. Letters tell our stories in such an evocative and interpersonal way, so that combination of personal record and history is chockful of such interesting events and information, palpably attached to the historical records of our psyches. My favorite epistolary writer is Emily Dickinson who said, "Nature is a haunted house. Art is a house that tries to be haunted." Perhaps it is the daily ghosts that we are trying to exhume in letters, in looking at the details of life, where we can also examine the lay of the land. I used to wait for the mailman, plonking in the snow with a daily talisman—something handwritten and full of news. The messenger may have changed, but not the message: We will still use this form to express our innermost thoughts and feelings. In my poem, "Dear Art," I feel that the form helped me ask the question, address the spiritual nature of Art and confront my own fears and longing. Something about signing off also gives a formal sense of closure and engages the reader, as if they are in on the most intimate secret.

from *In the Field Between Us,* Molly McCully Brown and Susannah Nevison

These poems are part of a longer epistolary sequence called *In the Field Between Us,* a book that tackles questions of identity and belonging in the aftermath of lifelong medical intervention. The book arose organically out of our conversations, and the collection depends on the epistolary form to place two voices in sustained, intimate discussion: each voice relies on the answering voice as both impetus and echo, and together they comprise not only a dialogue, but a landscape and a body all their own, where language binds and yokes the voices to each other as tightly as muscle, sinew, and bone. In this excerpt, the speakers imagine a space where they begin to break the bounds of their individual bodies and inhabit more fully the wild possibilities of the collective world they've built. The kinetic energy of the epistolary form propels the sequence forward, engendering a sense of companionship where there was once isolation.

"Postcards to Etheridge Knight," Todd Fuller

The inception of "Postcards to Etheridge Knight" occurred one night while my family and I were driving from Norman, Oklahoma to Pawnee, Oklahoma. As we approached Perkins, a small rural, I noticed a sign, "Etheridge Ranch" and immediately thought of my former teacher. I exclaimed, "*Etheridge!,*" startling everyone in the car. My son, four at the time, retorted, "Don't yell in the car Daddy," and then asked, "Who is Etheridge?" The poem provides a few answers to my son's question. Twenty-five years after his death, Etheridge is eulogized through an epistolary poem generated by my son's inquisitive nature. I chose to write a postcard poem as a response to a letter Etheridge wrote me—the one I never got to answer because of his death to cancer. It made the most sense to honor Etheridge via postcard poems with a blues-style, call-and-response structure.

"Letter to Hillary on the Radical Hospitality of the Body," Erika Meitner

In the spring of 2017, I started corresponding with a millennial poet named Hillary Adler, who's in her mid-twenties and lives in New York City, which is where I grew up, and where I lived in my twenties. I am in my early forties, and live in rural Southwest Virginia, which is where Hillary grew up and went to college. We've been sending poem-letters back and forth for nearly two years now, offering each other advice on how to move through our respective landscapes, our lives as women, and our quarter-life and mid-life crises. Our letter-poems are diffuse, but they often talk about poetry, politics, desire, technology, and our bodies. For part of July 2017, I was in residency at the Virginia Center for the

Creative Arts. The first night I got to the artists' colony, everyone was having a dance party in an abandoned barn. I hadn't danced in years, and everything detailed in this epistolary poem is precisely true, including the complications of sealing ourselves off from the outside world to make art; the world keeps finding its way in, electronically, bodily, through objects and sounds, messages and signs.

"After the Dragonflies," Chris Green

All of my poems are ghost-epistles—secret letters to everyone I've ever known. In poems, I say what I couldn't have said, or didn't, or can't say still. This one is a poem to my dear brother about love and regret and distance, all dressed up in the strange memory of dragonflies on a summer's day.

"Postcard: Morning Window, Venice," Donna Masini

A postcard is a moment in time. *Now. Here. I think of you.* Even in the tiniest handwriting it's got to be brief. Perhaps under that "I wish you were here" cliché is the understanding that the moment is essentially untranslatable—which makes it like a poem. Because I often use them as bookmarks, I come upon these postcards years later, missives from a distant past, as when, last week, I pulled out the first volume of *In Search of Lost Time* and found a Seurat from my ex-husband. 1990, the first time I read Proust; cards from the (long gone) Endicott Bookshop; notes penciled on the backs and margins. Notes about the nature of time.

So *this* poem: I had drafts and fragments that hadn't gone into the manuscript I'd just turned in. One was an address to my sister, only one phrase of which moved me: "Were you not dead." The heartbreak of the subjunctive. The awful moment when you realize the only person who would "get it" is dead. When I was thirteen I read that Venice was dying and worried it would die before I got to see it. I've been to Venice three times. The image on this card is a photograph I took of an early morning when my sister was still alive. The postcard is an elegy to that time. To be in that room, at that time, would be to be back in a time before the loss.

POEMS IN FORM

"The Crux," Rosanna Warren

For several years I had been pondering a photograph of two arms extended through prison bars of separate cells to play a game of dominoes on the hallway floor. Neither man could see the other. I kept trying—and failing—to build a poem around it: the game seemed to mean either too much or too little. In yet another attempt, the poem started shaping into jagged quatrains, and I found myself imprisoning them in rhyme—something I've avoided recently. But it's a prison poem. At the same time, the syntax wanted to bust out of those constraints, and that seemed right. It was an accident that it turned into a sonnet: I didn't want to keep this dense metaphysical word game going any longer, since it threatened to overwhelm the subject. The Elizabethan final mousetrap couplet is not a move I usually make, not wanting to enforce such mortal closure. But this is a poem about death sentences. I hoped the mystery of the statement would undermine the apparent authority of the couplet form.

"How To:", Jordi Alonso

"How To:", from its title on, looks to lay out the basics of sonnet-writing in the form of an English sonnet. The idea of poets receiving (as if from some muse) ideas for poems while on walks is quite cliché, even more so when moonlight is involved—but, the genesis of this sonnet happened to be one of those moments for me. I had gone out for a walk late one night, and the line "A fourteenth of a sonnet is now done" slipped into my head. Building on that line, I continued describing the component parts of an English sonnet. I particularly enjoyed writing the self-referential asides in lines 6 to 10, which lead to the heroic couplet that ends "How to" on a slightly irreverent—yet formally-appropriate—line.

"Reckoning," Jeanetta Calhoun Mish

This poem arrived as an unrhymed, unmetered Shakespearean sonnet of three quatrains and a concluding slant-rhymed couplet. Once I'd written the first draft, I realized the poem wanted more structure—but not necessarily structure by rhyme. As I revised, I counted each line and saw that each line held close to fourteen syllables, which reminded me of the "fourteener," a line of seven iambic feet, used in Greek and Latin prosody and revived in Elizabethan verse. I revised each line to equal fourteen syllables while choosing not to force it into iambic feet as was the past practice. Therefore, this poem doesn't scan to a standard meter. I also decided that, in order to move the fourteener into the 21st century, I shouldn't concern myself with overall rhyme or the traditional caesura (a break or pause in the line) at the eighth syllable. However, there are several lines where caesuras organically appeared. Perhaps my ear's preference for the fourteener line was influenced by my love of ballads—contemporary and ancient. When two fourteener lines are divided into two lines of eight and two of six syllables, the resulting stanza becomes standard ballad meter.

"Haiku," Molly Peacock

It was only at America's hundredth birthday party, the 1876 Centennial Exhibition in Philadelphia, that citizens first saw items of Japanese design.

In poetry there also existed in Japan a stanza form that was inspiringly simple—but also many-layered in the way it evoked response. It was the classical Japanese tradition of hokku. The three-line verse is comprised of five, then seven, then five Japanese moras or Western language syllables. Revered poets Basho (1644–94), Buson (1716–84) and Issa (1763–1828) practiced this tradition for centuries. But just around the time that Americans were discovering Japanese design, the classical forms of poetry were being rejuvenated in Japan. Around the turn of the 20th century the poet Shiki (1867–1902) renamed the three-line form "haiku." As Shiki resuscitated the form in Japan, it inspired interest among Western poets first in France, then in Spain and Latin America and in North America, especially Imagist poets Amy Lowell and Ezra Pound. In the mid 20th century, after World War II, North Americans took an even greater interest in Zen Buddhism, and in the vision on aging through nature, that the haiku offers.

Haiku are fun because they're small. They look easy, but I rewrote this one many times. I had to get the sense of that spider with its own life, knowing what it was doing, using that yoga mat for an entirely different purpose than a human would. Is the spider the yoga teacher? Another question: isn't it time to stop saying you don't have time to write? You *always* have time for three lines.

"The UFO Incident," Tony Trigilio

I began this poem as I do all sestinas, with an automatic writing exercise to sketch out an opening stanza and identify the sestina end-words. But each effort to draft a foundational stanza produced only flat language and predictable end-words. Everything changed when I sat down, pen and notebook in hand, for my third re-watching of *The UFO Incident*, the made-for-TV movie that is the poem's subject matter. This time, I found myself transfixed by the film's introductory text as it scrolled up the screen in melodramatic all-caps: "THE FOLLOWING STORY IS BASED ON THE RECORDS OF THE UNITED STATES AIR FORCE, THE FILES OF THE HAYDEN PLANETARIUM AND THE ACTUAL TRANSCRIPTS OF THE TAPES MADE BY BETTY AND BARNEY HILL, UNDER HYPNOSIS, BY DR. BENJAMIN SIMON. . . . " I paused and rewound constantly, building the first stanza around these opening words as they scrolled hypnotically up the screen. Eventually, I realized this stanza actually should function as an epigraph (as it does in the movie), forecasting the sestina's narrative while introducing its end-words to the reader. From there, I built each successive stanza around this one, varying the end-words so that their repetition would be musically dynamic. The poem is indebted to Jeffery Conway, whose poetry collection, *Showgirls: The Movie in Sestinas*, was my inspiration for applying the venerable poetic form of the sestina to a low-budget, kitschy, made-for-TV movie.

"Villanelle of Margaritas," Allison Joseph

Villanelles, for me, are connected to my first becoming a poet. After first reading Sylvia Plath's *The Bell Jar*, I skipped to the novel's afterword and discovered her poem "Mad Girl's Love Song." Those refrains! This poem, written when Plath was not much older than my then-adolescent self, haunted me. It was my first time seeing the form, though I didn't attempt one right away. I was too intimidated. It would be years before I wrote one.

I once began a villanelle with the refrain line "What fool would write a villanelle?" Over and over, I've been that fool. I've written dozens and dozens of villanelles for practice, searching for just the right twist on a refrain line, feeling annoyed with myself when I pick an end word that doesn't have enough rhyme partners. The form intoxicates me, seduces me, leaves me crying after elusive refrains and distraught for the world. Perhaps that's a bit of an exaggeration, but I do find myself circling back to the villanelle frequently, as I strive to write a poem that will please my innate sense of repetition, my penchant for rhyme, and my desire for musicality.

"Ballad of the Bronx Zoo's Beloved," Judith Baumel

A ballad tells a shocking or tragic story in song. It is voiced by an anonymous narrator reporting a scene with quoted and repeated speech. Ballads usually use quatrains shaped by a rhyme scheme and their lines usually have four (sometimes three or five) feet. At the end of the 19th century, in his master-collection *English and Scottish Popular Ballads*, Harvard professor James Francis Child identified 305 oral folk ballad templates still in circulation. Literary ballads are another thing. They are self-consciously artful constructions of literate voices and often refract contemporary anxieties through dual prisms of tradition and change. Think of the *Lyrical Ballads* by Coleridge and Wordsworth. Think of all the Romantics and think of their children, grandchildren and so on, down to us.

In this poem I used quoted speech from a nursery rhyme, the form of which is a variation on a ballad. What's the tragic story here? The first gorilla born in the New York City was named Pattycake, in a contest sponsored by the *New York Daily News*. When Pattycake was six months, her mother Lulu and father Kongo pulled her from opposite sides of the cage and broke her arm. From that moment she was the zoo's most popular attraction. Pattycake grew up to have 10 children including the identical twins Ngoma and Tambo. She died at age 40 as "The Bronx Zoo's Beloved," having lived a brutal, public life.

"The Summer Before the Student Murders," Randall Mann

"The Summer Before the Student Murders" is written in catalectic lines—in this case, headless dimeter: the first unstressed syllable is dropped in each line to achieve a sharpening effect, which I hope creates and supports the tragicomic content of the poem. I left out punctuation in part to have the lines unmoored on the page, much like fragments in memory. (The formal inspiration for this poem is Tim Dlugos's "The Bar.") I grew up in Florida; this poem alludes to certain details about the summer I spent in Orlando in 1990, prior to going to the University of Florida. When I arrived at college, on the first day of class, a serial killer began murdering students. I wanted to capture something about that odd, humid time before the murders, which seemed full of promise, and, in hindsight, perhaps marked something like the beginning of menace, and the end of innocence, too.

"Departures," Emma Bolden

I first learned about French repeating forms in high school. I felt fascinated and frustrated by the way these forms worked through revolution rather than resolution. I studied how other writers used refrain to build a structure that allowed in a kind of meaning that moved beyond causality, chronology, and the comfort of a "happily ever" ending. I could not, however, find a door through which to walk with my own work into these forms. A coincidence saved me: my best friend, an ice skater, showed me a tape of Torvill and Dean's 1984 Olympic routine, choreographed to Maurice Ravel's "Boléro." In the movement of the music and of their bodies, in the circles their skates traced into the ice and that final, frenetic fall, I understood refrain not as rote repetition but as transformation, as a way to see the motifs of meaning in our lives as cycles that bring great joy and great pain. That music, that moment, returned to me nearly twenty years later, as I stood watching the highway after another love had entered and exited my life. There was no way to write that love and loss but through refrain.

"Vivid Isolation: A Ghazal," Tina Chang

Any ghazal I write is a tribute to my dear teacher, the late Agha Shahid Ali. I first experienced Shahid when I was an undergraduate student at Binghamton University. In his unforgettable poetry workshop, he introduced me to the seventh-century Arabic form and I couldn't help but feel he was largely responsible for making the form popular to western audiences via his anthology, *Ravishing Disunities: Real Ghazals in English* (Wesleyan University Press, 2000). The ghazal is one of the most perfect verse forms as it relies on all the tools a poet should master: prosody, rhythm, rhyme, repetition, compression, efficiency, tension, and freedom. Often the themes of the ghazal focus on religion, love, loss, romantic longing, and pain. The ghazal is comprised of at least five couplets with a word of refrain which appears at the end of each line in the opening couplet (*matla*) and at the end of the second line in succeeding couplets (*radif*). Every word of refrain is immediately preceded by a rhyme (*qafia*). Each couplet works on its own as an independent thought as well as in conversation with the other couplets in the ghazal. Shahid liked to think of the stanzas as stones in a necklace that shined in "vivid isolation," which became the title of my ghazal. The most wondrous and thrilling aspect of the ghazal is the reference to the author's own name by poem's end which serves as a meditation, prayer, and calling. I took the liberty to sound out, not my own name, but Shahid's. This is my homage to him, a thunderclap of his ongoing voice.

"World Gone Wrong," William Wadsworth

This poem was inspired by a poem in Peter Cole's anthology, *The Dream of the Poem: Hebrew Poetry from Muslim and Christian Spain*, "World Gone Wrong," by Shelomo Bonafed, who wrote in the late fifteenth century. The poem is dedicated to Agha Shahid Ali, a Muslim poet from Kashmir who moved to the U.S. and wrote in English, and to Umair Kazi—writers whose works have forged connections between Eastern and Western cultures. I'm drawn to the Bonafed poem's four-beat meter and its formal structure, which, though not divided into quatrains, easily could have been, as evidenced in the first four lines quoted inside my poem. In English literature, the four-square rhymed quatrain, whether the lines are consistently four-beat or alternate in lines of four and three (or just two) beats, has its roots in Old English and the oral tradition. The longer iambic pentameter line and fancier stanzaic models came later, when Chaucer and the Elizabethans brought French, Italian and classical Greek and Latin models into English poetry. But from Coleridge and Keats, to Tennyson and Dickinson, to Frost, Auden, Larkin, Walcott and Heaney, the lyrical possibilities of this primordial form have been continually renewed by the more modern poets I most admire.

from "Frolic and Detour," Paul Muldoon

This is the first third of a longish poem entitled "Frolic and Detour," a term with a very specific meaning in tort law. It seems a detour occurs when an employee makes a "minor" departure from his employer's charge while a frolic is a "major" departure that happens when the employee is acting for his own benefit. It struck me that this hairsplitting over major and minor forms of side-tracking might be a fun way of thinking not only about how some lives get lived but about how some poems get made. In the case of this one, it makes a very recognizable shape in the world. That's to say it's written in quatrains. And *that*'s another way of saying it's written in very long couplets, the couplet being at the heart of so many versification projects from Chaucer to Chance the Rapper. This phenomenon of the rhyming couplet is often seen as some form of constraint—the word being in bondage!—rather than being intrinsic to how language functions. The real constraint in "Frolic and Detour" is much more profound; it's a poem that uses the same ninety rhyme words, in the same order, as half a dozen other longish poems I've written over the last twenty years.

PERSONA POEMS

"Buckle and Wash," John A. Nieves

After a conversation with one of my students double-majoring in creative writing and environmental studies about sea-level rise claiming islands in the Chesapeake, I did some research on these islands. After reading some scholarly accounts, some newspaper articles, and a few stray factoids, I found a small article with pictures on Atlas Obscura about the disappearance of Holland Island. The pictures, especially one of a crumpling family home, stirred me. Imagined the people who had lived there and what they would think now. Many of the sources cited 1914 as the year erosion first deeply attacked the island. I chose the year before that to imagine a child dreaming the future so I could answer my own curiosity in someone else's voice. I needed to know what slow-motion tragedy would look like when viewed from one moment. I needed to hear the voice that could speak it. I chose wobbling tercets to capture the unease of the child, the steadiness of the father, the folly in such steadiness. I wanted readers to hold both times in their own mouths on the tongue of this phantom child.

"From My Lord's Estate, I Pass High Mountains, Winding Streams, Rocky Torrents, Thick Forests, and Tall Bamboo," Sebastian Bitticks

This poem began as an exercise to imagine a poet writing in another tradition, and then write a translation of his or her work. I found myself in familiar territory, since the first poems I read seriously were all translations of classics from Japan and China. Partly, it was the language I loved: hard as marbles in the mouth, clacking around an obstinate original. To my young ear, those poems suggested a limit to what could be done in my own language, a fact both liberating and discomforting. Today I write a lot of persona poems, and I think of all of them as imaginary translations, even when the subject is Anglophone. I'm less looking for a voice to inhabit than a gap: between what could be said in another time and what feels native to the present. Like the translations that were so formative to me, I hope for language that is barely holding together, that strains across a divide. The speaker of this poem, a poet's chief of staff written out of history, would not have recognized himself as a creative force, only as a go-between. It's how I wanted to feel about writing him.

"Sole Heiress," Joan Houlihan

The poem's I is a balm, a conceit, an expectation of truth, and a belief in the unity of self. A persona poem, however, can use the I to open into the Other and achieve the kind of honesty only a mask allows. Anonymity enables truth-telling. After reading some Jungian case studies from a hospital in Switzerland, I wanted to let one of the most intriguing patients speak through the I of my poem. She was a turn-of-the century, schizophrenic, elderly woman from a wealthy family in Switzerland with a striking voice and puzzling point of view—as far away from my "real" self as could be. My interest in her motivation, background, passions and suffering drove my creation of the I in this poem; and, in its exploration of her existential loneliness, the poem turned out to have much more to do with me, the poet, than I knew. The mask as revealer!

"Laloo, the Handsome, Healthy, Happy Hindoo," Ravi Shankar

Wearing a mask allows us to reveal a side of ourselves we might not otherwise see, or indeed let others see. Writing in the long tradition of the persona poem, which has as its adherents such poets as Shakespeare, Browning, Hughes, and Ai, I decided to take on the voice of the fascinating and too-little known historical personage, Laloo the Healthy, Handsome, Happy Hindoo, who toured with Barnum & Bailey. My own identification with this figure began with a birthday gift from a friend of an awfully un-politically correct, but nonetheless transfixing, set of playing cards. The pack included bearded fire-eaters, angry dwarves and three-legged men, all from the circus past of American history. It also included Laloo.

Laloo, with his parasitic twin brother emerging misshapen from his chest, smiled a regal benediction. He seemed to possess soul, what we call *jīvana* in India, inner fire; plus, he was Indian and to be frank, I felt back then about my Indian heritage the way he seemed to feel about his deformed sibling. I decided to use the form of rhyming quatrains to express the formality and stateliness of Laloo's life, for though derided as a freak, he also saw more of the world than anyone from his homeland and became a brief American success story. Writing this poem allowed me to access my own childhood memories while delving into the biographical details of Laloo's own remarkable life as an activist and performer.

"Pity Eyed," Marilyn Nelson

In September 2017, I was driving from the Nashville airport to Sewanee, TN, to meet friends for dinner at The University of the South and give a reading the following day. It was late afternoon. There was a lot of traffic. From a distance I saw a pickup truck on the shoulder of the highway, and people standing on it, waving their arms. I pulled over. I had misgivings as soon as I saw the stringy-haired skinny young white guy who ran up. He said they'd run out of gas and his cell phone was dead, that they'd been trying to flag down someone for 45 minutes, and I was the first person who had stopped. Nervously, I drove him and the woman with him to the next gas station. He told me he had agreed to meet his girlfriend, who was getting out of rehab, at a Walmart down the road. He was going to be late; his phone wasn't working, so he couldn't call her. Weeks later, I told this story to a workshop I was leading and someone suggested I write about the girlfriend waiting at Walmart.

"This River," Elizabeth Macklin

This is the first conscious persona poem I ever wrote, as a section of a long reportage poem, "With Love from Ainezalandia." The first lines—"I'm 50 million now / and yesterday, // 50 thousand years ago, / your people came // to live by me, / to live and stay"—are a literal translation of the opening of Gaizka Aranguren's 2010 ecological documentary, *Ni, Bidasoa* (I, the Bidasoa). (Available online here: https://vimeo.com/41127954 and with Spanish subtitles here: https://vimeo.com/31498994). The rest comes loosely from the soundtrack and from contemplating the pictures on the screen. The Bidasoa river is the dividing line between Spain and France; the Basque Country straddles it. Thanks to Ainara Maia Urrotz for sending me the original link. The phrase *"water from hand to hand"* is from "Mendian gora" (Up the mountain; 1983), by Xabier Amuriza, which I first heard sung by Imanol Larzabal (1947–2004) in 2001, and subsequently translated for Mikel Urdangarin's 2017 version, on *Margolaria* (The Painter).

"Sparrow," January Gill O'Neil

For the past few years, I have been trying to write more observational poems. I'm fascinated by writing in the moment, and writing about the ordinary world. On a rainy morning, I looked out at my driveway and saw a sparrow preening in a puddle. I was just fascinated by this sparrow's contentment; I scribbled a few lines and wrote a draft few days later. It took a few attempts to create the staggered stanza, which began as a way of revising. Sometimes I see meaning better if I stagger the lines, hence, the form.

"The Language of the Bomb," Kimberly Grey

I wrote this poem while I was a winter fellow at Civitella Ranieri, a 15th century castle-turned-artist residency in rural Italy. It was the middle of the night when news broke that Trump had ordered the dropping of the largest non-nuclear bomb, nicknamed MOAB (or "mother of all bombs") in Afghanistan. I was all alone at the castle, awake from jet-lag, and felt paralyzed by this egregious and pompous show of unnecessary military force and spectacle. An immediate feeling of separateness overtook me: this "me/us" versus "them". I did not consent to this action. Many of us did not consent. It was then that the authorial distance necessary when embodying a persona was established. I thought to myself, what if the bomb itself also did not consent? What if it is an empathetic object? What would it say? It is humans who weaponize language and objects. Humans who construct things to purposefully destroy each other. The decision to let the bomb speak came from an overwhelming feeling of helplessness, of wanting to show the violence of the "they" who radicalize the object so that it becomes the evil thing. A transfer of responsibility. In this case, the thing that kills is not the real killer. I wanted to give the bomb the ability to transfer that violence back to where it belongs.

"Rescue Annie," Laura Kasischke

I wrote "Rescue Annie" after reading that the face of the mannequin used to teach CPR—that sandbag like doll that ends up on the floor of the gymnasium or at the front of the classroom, the one used by the Red Cross and others to train us in mouth-to-mouth resuscitation—was modeled after the deathmask of an "of an unidentified young woman reputedly drowned in the River Seine around the late 1880s." (Wikipedia). She's referred to as "the most kissed girl in the world" and also "the Mona Lisa of the Seine." I recalled my own CPR training, and my attempts to resuscitate that mannequin—first, per my instructor's directions, by shaking her and saying, "Annie, Annie: are you okay?"—so that, as with so many of my persona poems, the poem ended up being about me. Still, I wanted to imagine the story she would tell, too—both the drowned girl, and the mannequin. I've since glimpsed some suggestions that this story of the CPR mannequin's face, and the serene beauty of the unknown drowned girl's deathmask having been the inspiration for it, debunked. But, I choose to stay off Snopes and, with this as well as so many other things in my life, to stick with the romantic and eerie possibility of the legend instead of learning some dull truth. I want to believe that there are hundreds and thousands of us, from camp counselors and Boy Scouts to firefighters and medical school students, perpetually bent over her, shaking (gently, per instructions) that girl found floating so long ago in the Seine, asking her if she's okay, and trying again and again to save her.

"One Hundred Umbrellas," David Yezzi

This dramatic monologue is spoken in the voice of the French avant-garde composer Erik Satie (1866–1925). As the poem suggests, he possessed many eccentricities, including a diet of all white food and a propensity for hoarding. In 1893, Satie fell in love with the painter Suzanne Valadon. Though the affair was short-lived, it was Satie's most significant romantic relationship. Valadon refused marriage but took an apartment next to Satie on the Rue Cortot in the Montmartre neighborhood of Paris. Satie composed music for her, calling her his *Biqui*. When Valadon moved away after six months, she left behind a now-famous portrait of the composer. Satie was devastated. Poverty forced him to move to the Paris suburb of Arcueil. At his death, his cramped apartment there overflowed with objects he had gathered, including a hundred umbrellas. In the poem, Satie appears to be speaking to a woman as she changes into one of Suzanne's gowns, but in the end he is left only with his disappointed imaginings. I was first drawn to the subject by Satie's well-known piano composition, *Gymnopedie No. 1,* which carries the notation *lent et doloreux* ("slow and dolorous"). This piece, for solo piano, always reminds me of a cold spring rain.

MYTH POEMS

"The Love Song of the Kraken," Martín Espada

This is a poem in the voice of a creature so feared that fear invented him. The mythological beast encounters a single human being who is unafraid, dispelling misconceptions about his species by demonstrating what he has in common with humans: the capacity to give and receive love. Of course, the poem revels in the absurd juxtapositions of the imagined human-kraken relationship, from the sea monster bursting into song to strolling on the boardwalk with his beloved. This poem owes a debt to Lucille Clifton and "the yeti poet returns to his village to tell his story," a work that speaks in the voice of another mythological creature to challenge our flawed perspectives. On one level, this poem celebrates the transcendence of fear so overwhelming that we cannot see what we see. On a more immediate, intimate level, this is a love poem written by one real person for another real person, an expression of praise and gratitude—and a birthday present, read aloud for the occasion.

"Assos," Christopher Bakken

The coastal town of Assos, Turkey, is located on the same peninsula as the city of Troy. The ramparts of Assos are crowned by the ruins of a Temple of Athena—if you stand in those ruins, the Greek island of Lesvos is visible just across a narrow strait. Few spots on the planet are as saturated with mythic resonance and no seaway has inspired as much legend—since Homeric times, scenes of heroism and devastation have taken place on these waters. My poem certainly draws upon those layers of ancient significance, but I am trying to come to terms with a contemporary tragedy of mythic proportions. In the past five years, thousands of refugees fleeing war and persecution have drowned off the coast of Assos while attempting to reach Greece in small boats and rafts. Many of these refugees were women and children. In this poem, and in a companion poem called "Lesvos," I tried to capture the sense of enormity and powerlessness these discarded heroes have faced while searching for a new home, or some temporary shelter, or even just one safe harbor.

"Sleeping Woman," Duane Niatum

"Sleeping Woman" is a mysterious woman in the Klallam stories. She comes back from our earliest stories. In fact, the only things we know about her are her name and that she was a shaman who aroused the jealousy of the male shamans from all the Klallam villages. Historically, there were twenty-five villages on the Olympic Peninsula and five villages on Vancouver Island. Today, only three villages exist. The male shamans were determined to sabotage her gifts so that the people would not take her medicine seriously. The woman who first told me "Sleeping Woman's story" is a Lower Elwha storyteller and teacher of the language. I was fascinated by the tidbits that my friend gave me and wrote a story first and then a poem based on that story. My job was to give Sleeping Woman a contemporary context and bring in our youth that have distanced themselves from the language and ancient stories. I try to show the shaman needs to be remembered and respected even when she doesn't fit the stereotype.

"Composition," John A. Nieves

This poem unspooled over the course of a year. I was asked at a reading in Delaware a strange formulation of a usual question. A woman in the front row asked, *Can you think of an event from your childhood that made you into a poet?* I gave her a weak, off-the-cuff answer about reading poetry as a child. It was true, but I knew it wasn't it. Over the next few weeks, this question dogged me. I went back to childhood memories of death and moving and Challenger, but none of those answers felt true either. Then, while thumbing through a coffee-table book on world mythologies, I remembered doing the same as a child. I remembered my friend and her missing cat. I wrote down everything I could summon about the event—three single-spaced pages of prose. This was my origin myth. This felt true. Over the next nine months, I whittled those pages down into this poem. I needed long lines and repetition. I needed narrative and ritual. I needed this mythology to make my own present whole.

"Transit of Venus," Stefanie Wortman

In my daughter's room, there is a formidable wooden rocking chair with blue upholstery on the padded seat and back. We inherited it from my husband's family. It was where his mother rocked him as a baby, and I spent a lot of time after our first child was born sitting in that chair, the floor around it getting speckled with white. I had been warned, by real women and by the Milky Way myth, that breast milk shoots out forcefully. Still I was surprised and amazed by the effect. I was also surprised and amazed by my baby. I expected her to be tender and fragile, and she was, but she was also incredibly strong, and fierce. When she flailed her tiny arms, I felt like she was fighting me, or waging a more comprehensive battle against the world I had brought her into. A sign at the children's museum where I take her now says a baby is stronger, pound for pound, than an ox. So, while the breast milk made me think of the Hera myth, it informed, too, my thinking about my Hercules baby, who seemed not like the soft and sweet offspring of Love, but like a little brawler who would take on anything.

"Made / Maeve 1," Leah Umansky

This poem is inspired by HBO's *Westworld*, and is part of a poetic sequence. In the television show, humans live in an imagined future where they can enter Westworld, and live out their fantasies with engineered robots passing as "humans." Maeve mysteriously gains consciousness, and her creator, Ford, wants to wipe her clean and to erase her suffering, so that she can continue as the brothel's madam. Maeve is trying to understand her memories. She is on a quest for identity and for power. I wrote this poem because it often feels that our lives are made up of other peoples' stories, especially for women. In this poem, the speaker identifies with and feels for Maeve. Both feel lost in their worlds and often burdened by the desires of men. Maeve wants to know her truth, but her experiences are maneuvered by the Westworld technicians. This poem's genesis started in dystopia, moved through myths like Pygmalion and then shifted into the present day. Maeve is a heroine of her own life and she's creating her own story. I love that.

"The Damned," Kevin Prufer

I've been writing about winged people for many years now, trying to imagine what happens when that element of myth—an element loaded with symbolic significance—intrudes on our everyday lives. Often, I try to recreate a consciousness that, though surrounded by the mythic, seems unwilling or unable to acknowledge its existence. In this poem, the rather unimaginative speaker meditates on the collapse of everything he knows, and the eventual rebirth of his city—without really seeming to understand the wildness of his own story, the significance of the winged people, the fact that he is writing from within a sort of circular foundation myth. I wonder, rereading this poem, if part of this speaker's winglessness is internal to himself, not a question of salvation in the usual sense, but the salvation imagination or myth offer us in the face of what might be horrifying or incredible.

"Shade," Richard Tillinghast

"Shade" brings together several energy strands. About the Metaphysical Poets of 17th century England, Samuel Johnson wrote: "The most heterogeneous ideas are yoked by violence together," and that happens here, but without violence—though the points of disjunction are meant to be jarring. I really do think it is "a fine thing" to do nothing, and I enjoyed evoking that river shaded by cottonwoods out West somewhere. Let's talk myth: I grew up in the Bible-reading South where engaging fancifully and irreverently with biblical stories came naturally, to me at least. Adam and Eve were as familiar as your first cousins. I like God marking his place in a book with his index finger; this God is a fallible character who evolves—"eager to learn" after all—so why shouldn't he be reading a mythical book out of a doo-wop song from the late 50s? (We assume he listens to the radio.) I read the Hesiod quote in some magazine, and it proved to be the poem's crucial turning point—from meditative quietness to expulsion from the garden. Eve is out of Lucas Cranach the Elder's painting in Pasadena. I'll pass over Adam, the snake, and the first poem without comment.

"At the Expulsion," Edward Hirsch

T. S. Eliot coined the phrase *mythical method* to refer to the way that a modern writer, such as James Joyce, employs a myth in a contemporary work, "manipulating a continuous parallel between contemporaneity and antiquity." That's a little grand for my unpunctuated sonnet, a love poem, but it makes the point that it's possible to find a parallel between a contemporary experience and an ancient story. Sometimes one turns to the myths, to archetypal stories, to try to understand one's own experience. You trust the wisdom of the original story and use it to get at something that's otherwise unavailable to you. There are many reasons why the story of Adam and Eve continues to resonate, especially for lovers, but one of them is that the movement or fall from paradise into time is irreversible. I thought I'd see what happened if I imagined my cheeky troublemaker as the original woman in the Garden.

"Eve Speaks," Grace Schulman

Myth is a wonderful method for art. It implies that human nature never changes. When the Bible is read as myth, not as literal fact, its characters reveal our own thoughts and desires. And despite hundreds of commentaries over the years, like many great poems, the bible remains open to interpretation.

I imagine Adam couldn't speak at the height of emotion, and instead found his voice in public declamations. The Bible has other instances of inarticulate responses, among them David's bareness of utterance when hearing that his son, Absalom is dead. In my poem, Adam's naming things leads to naming abstractions, and as he becomes obsessed with designations, he develops the hubris of finding words for human frailties, the universe, even God. Frightened of what he's done, he falls silent.

I wanted to get inside the minds of man and wife to understand their private responses to Adam's work. But intentions are beside the point. Reading it now, I see that my poem changed its course. It's really about the dual power and limitations of language.

EKPHRASIS

"Vanitas," Mary Jo Salter

Vanitas paintings draw me by their frank, often witty signals that not only the artist but the artwork will die. And the trompe-l'oeil decay of this Flemish canvas, the decrepit-painting-within-intact-painting examined in my poem "Vanitas," is full of such lively self-awareness. That said, the artist was dead to me, even unborn to me, before I looked him up. He had the funny name of Cornelis Norbertus Gysbrechts, he was "active" from 1657-1675, and the full title of his little-known but excellent painting is "Trompe l'oeil Studio Wall with a Vanitas Still Life." I happened upon it in one of the world's most famous museums, The National Gallery of London, but it was "on loan" (aren't we all?). Its home is a gallery in Hull, a city I might never have mentioned had it not rhymed with "skull," a word for the object that is the painting's centerpiece. A rhyme often starts a poem for me—usually a verbal rhyme but sometimes a visual one. And the visual rhyme that also got this poem going is the likeness of the two voids the painting records: the artist's palette, a tool for affirming colorful life, has a thumb-hole in it like the gray skull's eye-hole. I wouldn't have caught that in a lesser painter's work, and catching it made me feel more alive, more like an artist who needed to make something. Forgive me, Mr. Gysbrechts, for not giving the full title of your painting in my poem, where I also pretend not to remember who you are. But didn't you invite me, or some other forgettable person, to go on asserting that you'll be forgotten?

"Laundry," Kwame Dawes

"Laundry" is a peculiar sliver of verse whose economy is dictated to by the photograph, "The Couple", a brilliantly named and executed photo by Mexican photographer, Graciela Iturbide, in her stunning book, *Eyes to Fly With*. Why describe it? I have already limited it by associating it with this poem, because the poem is not *about* the photograph, but what happens when one stares at a photo and discovers that it is crowded in language, whipping stories, ideas, and moods. I have learned to sieve these "noises" through my peculiar filter, to produce poems. The cheat is the title of the photograph: "The Couple". It is brilliant. Iturbide has caught the poem of clothes hanging from an outdoor clothes line in Panama City, Panama. I am the interloper, the pilferer, the one who dashes away with a stolen poem. But I am good at this, so good that she has not missed it.

"Terra Nova: Juno Gemes," Forrest Gander

Juno Gemes is one of Australia's most notable photographers, documenting the changing social landscape of Australia. In particular, she records the lives and struggles of Aboriginal Australians, a process that culminated in her being selected in 2008 as one of ten photographers invited to document the National Apology in Canberra. She has collaborated on books and editorial projects with her partner, the renowned Australian poet Robert Adamson. In 2008, when I visited both of them in their home, Gemes was working on a series exploring early European "encounters" with aboriginal Australia. She asked me if I would write something to accompany the photographs. I took notes, but the poems only developed years later. This is the first of them to be published. The lineation acts out a kind of tentative territorial exploration; the language, dissatisfied with dispassionate description, invests the landscape with psychic qualities that make a critique, but don't make that critique easy. The most potent force in the image as in the poem is what remains invisible.

"Photograph of Two Young Couples with One Person Missing," Michael Collier

While our lives are dynamic, always in motion and difficult to arrest, a photograph, especially a personal photograph, suspends a moment and allows us to imagine ourselves as we once were. Photographs, like most works of art, create tension between a past moment, the present, and the future's gravitational pull. All of this tension resides in the viewer. The drama of ekphrasis—the work about the work of art—is to give life to this tension by creating a parallel experience, one that is often speculative. The moral of ekphrasis, if there is one, is that art begets art. Rilke's "Portrait of My Father as a Young Man," "Corpse Washing," and "The Carousel" serve as models for mine. "Portrait of My Father as a Young Man" is clearly ekphrastic, but Rilke finds in the scenes of women washing a corpse and young girls riding a carousel the *drama* of ekphrasis, and so by a reverse transformative power his poems invite us to think of those activities as works of art. In my poem, I've tried to make space in the photograph for the photographer and her missing presence.

"Ascension," Grace Schulman

When I first gazed at Christ rising to Heaven in the mural by John LaFarge, the altarpiece in Ascension Church, I wanted to cry out in wonder. Looking up at the painting, I had a vision of Japan: a Kyoto garden, a whiff of kirinmaru peony. What were they doing in the Episcopal church on lower Fifth Avenue in New York? Highly unlikely, because the environs are characteristically American, from the Tiffany windows and sculptured angels by Saint Gaudens to the original top-hat congregation. After I wrote the poem, still baffled by the incongruity, I read in a book called *The Great Wave* by Christopher Benfey, that La Farge had the same thought. When he agreed to paint the mural, uneasy after a troubled marriage, he left the country for Japan. He saw Mount Fuji, broke free from his block, and painted Christ wafting up from the Judean hills to Heaven. But was it the Judean hills? Or was it Mount Fuji, his source of inspiration and mine?

"Titian's *Marsyas*," Lloyd Schwartz

To quote Frank O'Hara, *I'm not a painter, I am a poet*, but I'm passionate about paintings. One I'm particularly obsessed with is Titian's *The Flaying of Marsyas,* his horrifying/ravishing image of the suffering inflicted on an artist who dares to compete with a god. In it, Titian paints himself as the unflinching eye-witness to the excruciating punishment. It's his tragic masterpiece—his *King Lear*—found in his studio when he died, at nearly 90. Was he still working on it, or could he just not bring himself to part with it? Its first transatlantic exhibit wasn't until 1986, at the National Gallery. I was floored, and have since traveled abroad to see it whenever I could. In 2016, it finally made it to New York—in the challenging/mind-expanding show called *Unfinished* that opened the new Met Breuer. This time, seeing it again—and again—and trying to hold as much of it as possible in my memory, I couldn't stop myself from writing about it.

"*The Flaying of Marsyas*," David Yezzi

Titian's masterpiece, painted shortly before his death in 1576, is sumptuous and horrible at the same time. It depicts the story of Marsyas, a satyr who loses a musical competition with Apollo and pays with his life. "Flaying," or skinning, was a painful form of execution in which the skin of the victim was removed. Titian's scene is one of enormous cruelty. But why was Marsyas punished in this way? Was it because he dared to challenge Apollo? Some versions of the story suggest that Apollo won unfairly, by adding his voice to the music of the pipes. What was it about Marsyas's virtuosity that so angered Apollo and that led him to remove Marsyas's music from the world? As in many ekphrastic poems, the painting raises questions that the poem tries to consider. This painting by Titian, available online, belongs to the National Museum in Kroměříž, in the Czech Republic. I saw it when it came to New York City in 2016 for the opening of the Met Breuer Museum.

"Notes on a Diebenkorn," Tess Taylor

When I look at the painting I write about in this poem, I see a Bay Area street caught late afternoon, blazing so brightly I can almost smell the tarmac and eucalyptus. It's as if there is an entire topography compressed into squares of color and light. Yet this is not a "place" per se. I have no idea what street it would be, and squinting, I can easily flatten the squares into abstract quilt pieces, or a grid-map seen from space. The painting is at once representational and abstract;

dimensional and flat. In particular, Diebenkorn's texture seems to create sense of place rather than place itself. He reminds us to remember how our own senses seem to assemble experience out of planes of color.

In writing this poem in response to a painting I have loved for years, I tried to puzzle out why I love this approach so much, and also to capture in my rhythm and syntax the bright and jumbled feeling of taking in the painting as a whole. This is a poem about pleasure as much as anything else. Just as a painting is neither representational or abstract, but somehow both at once, a poem is neither purely music or purely meaning but a combination of how these things interact to create the sensation of moving through thought and space. I suppose Diebenkorn's way of being specific-in-the-abstract (or using the abstract to hint at the specific) makes me remember not only to think about beauty but to ponder how beauty happens. "No ideas but in things," said William Carlos Williams. *No places but in colors*, Diebenkorn seems to reply. *No color but in light*.

"Shirt Noise," Christina Pugh

"Shirt Noise" treats a painting, but at several removes. Rather than providing a straightforward "study" of visual art, this poem discovers its ekphrastic identity along the path of its own unfolding. The poem's genesis was in its title; "shirt noise" was a phrase spoken one day by the producer of the *Poetry* magazine podcast that I record monthly with the other editors of the magazine. I was immediately taken with this phrase, and with the notion that the infinitesimal sound of a moving shirt might interfere with what the producer calls "room tone": the silence that he records for several seconds at the end of our talking. How often do we mark or curate silence at the end of an intellectual conversation? Yet this is what the recording technology both necessitates and enables. All of this led me to Jorie Graham's poem "Room Tone," but rather than focusing on the poem itself, I detoured, suddenly riveted by the image of Eric Fischl's painting on the book's cover, along with its relationship to the various silences both in that volume and inchoate in my own poem. Describing that image was a labor of love. But it was not where I expected or intended to be. For that reason, I suppose you could call this poem an "inductive ekphrasis."

"Allowing That," Karl Kirchwey

The ekphrastic poem has become a kind of contemporary literary fad, though the challenges of delivering a memorable poetic commentary on a visual original are considerable. I had known Marcel Duchamp to be an artist of significant and subversive wisdom, though I found some of his Dadaist experiments (a signed urinal, a snow shovel) gimmicky. Living outside of Philadelphia for many years, I was familiar with Duchamp's late masterpiece *Étant donnés*, an installation on which he worked for 25 years. The work's full title, which is in French, would translate as *Being Given: 1. The Waterfall 2. Gas for Lighting*, and apparently presents the terms of some exercise in logic, perhaps a syllogism. The title of my poem is intended to extend the satirical paradox of "allowing" or "being given" a logical structure for a content that seems to record an episode of sexual violence against a woman. My Bryn Mawr College colleague Jane Hedley had asked me to contribute to an anthology of essays about women poets and ekphrasis, so at the time I began this poem, I had been thinking about the power dynamics of the male gaze. Duchamp's work forces the viewer to peep through a barn door, assuming the role of voyeur. My poem ranges through a catalogue of names of real-life women who served as models for male artists such as Tintoretto, Botticelli, Titian, Manet, and Courbet (Duchamp's own model was Brazilian sculptor Maria Martins, with whom he was romantically involved), and emerges as an indictment of the male viewer himself. One of the leading exponents of an artistic movement susceptible to charges of misogyny, Duchamp may or may not have had such a self-critique in mind.

"Hic Adelfia Clarissima Femina," Judith Baumel

"Here lies." This familiar tombstone formula is an invitation to view. It is also a reminder of the impossibility of true viewing, alluding, as it does, to the most fundamental matters of the body and the soul. What we *once* saw lies here, now decaying and out of view. What we needed and need to see is unseeable and maybe non-existent. The sarcophagus decorations of the early Christians illustrated their questions about the afterlife in the context of Bible stories on this theme. The Adelfia niche in the catacombs of San Giovanni in Siracusa, Sicily adds one more play to the tradition. Its words undo its images. In the large central medallion is a bas relief of a woman embracing a man, yet the funerary inscription makes clear only the woman is buried within. A most excellent woman, a most tender couple, an unexplained rupture.

AUBADES & NOCTURNES

"Aubade with Wolf Spider," Aimee Nezhukmatathil

Most good-byes in poetry are unwanted goodbyes. In most aubades, regret or lament usually perfume the stanzas and lines, but one of the many logistical beauties of writing an aubade is that the poet can play with the lexicon of the natural world as sunrise approaches in the poem. Couple that with what poet Edward Hirsch calls the "day-lit mind which bears the grief or burden of longing for what has been lost," and you've a unique map of how to navigate a farewell with a vocabulary perhaps not normally employed in other poems of departure.

When writing an aubade, think of it as a chance for a heightened sensory cocktail—just like what happens in real life when the world lightens into view and bird-noise or honks that signal animals and plants and people all over the world bending toward working and loving (and sighing) in the sun and into the night. For an aubade to truly have that dynamic shift from the night-lit mind to the "day-lit mind," try including elements from the natural world that can only be seen/smelled/heard at night. In "Aubade with Wolf Spider," the narrator establishes the mood of the goodbye within the first two couplets. The narrator wants to delay the parting, the "hunger" of the first line. The poem then moves through a catalog of the outdoors at night, to a daytime memory of finding a swell of bounty—fruit, dozens of spider hatchlings with the "you" who was left—and finally a different kind of swell—of insect bites to haunt the speaker who ultimately savors them as a prize.

"At Dawn," David Baker

I love listening at night when the rain falls on my roof and among the leaves of the many trees around my house. I love when the wind turns softly through the leaves or roars wildly there, deeply. But there's something even more eerie—early mornings in winter—when I waken to find something has happened in the night, during my sleep, and I never knew it. The snow makes sounds, of course, but rarely can we hear it. "At Dawn" steps off from a phrase from the great poet W. S. Merwin, from his poem "The Sound of It," and I think the phrasing of my poem is a little like waking early, shaking off the sleep, seeing and hearing in hesitant bits, rubbing one's eyes to the surprise of a radically altered landscape, to heavy new snow. The ten-syllable lines are guided and laden with white space, drifted in snowfall, bowing in the middle with caesura. The poem is made of the morning's first words, first light, the morning stutter. It is a poem about quiet, and intimacy. Who is ever there to hear it?

"Aubade," Elizabeth Scanlon

I love the idea of a morning song because it honors a different kind of love than we usually celebrate. When I was writing this poem, it occurred to me that the aubade's original indication of "lovers parting at daybreak" was in the youthful mode, the Romeo-and-Juliet, star-crossed sense. Those lovers are sneaking off to avoid getting caught. But writing an aubade of this domestic life interested me because we so often aren't on the same bed schedules for many other reasons as well—work, children, anxiety, binge-watching TV shows. I wanted to make a song of parting for the grown-ups, for the lovers who see all the bumps and snags in full daylight and will return to that bed anyway.

"Canebreak Love and Water," Maurice Manning

The tradition of the aubade entails the regretted arrival of morning and the necessary parting of two lovers, presuming there is something illicit about their togetherness. I wrote this poem for my wife, Amanda, one morning looking out at our small farm and imagining our little piece of land as it was originally—with native cane growing along the streamside. There must have been a notable density to the vegetation in the early days of settling Kentucky, and I wanted to imagine the vitality of that original moment and how it might have struck the settlers and what it might have meant to them. The poem is an effort to imagine how that originating moment might have allowed the early folks to feel blessed, and to imply something of that original blessing is with us still. I aim to re-plant the native cane in the little field beside our house and hope to see it thrive. Although this poem does not conform to the technical requirements of a sonnet, I intend it as a double-sonnet, composed in tetrameter rather than pentameter, with an eccentric approach to rhyme, which, to my mind, suits the broader concerns of the poem.

"Music for Attack Helicopter," Andrew Zawacki

Set at a back-seat taxi window, en route to Charles de Gaulle airport, "Music for Attack Helicopter" is less a morning song of two lovers parting than a dawn patrol track about anonymity and leaving. The once natural world has become a network of harnessed power, manufacturing equipment, and myriad modes of transport which—aerial, terrestrial, marine—are ruining the elements they rely on. At once animated and desiccated by capital, the unnamed city, in turn, is practically virtual, laid out like a video game, framed by imaging technologies that mediate, if not nullify, face-to-face encounter. The relationship of "I" with "myself" is especially imperiled by the estrangement effects of hypermodernity, and the speaker of this poem, hurrying from one infernal "non-place" to another, finds himself, as it were, losing himself. While the matinal scene is underwritten by writing—from ideograms to loan words, cursive to griffonage—as though the world were still, reassuringly, structured like a language, the acoustics are overlorded by a military apparatus. Speaking of ransacking spectral antecedents: I might have taken the title from a poem by contemporary French writer Dominique Fourcade.

"Nocturne for the Bereft," Mai Der Vang

I love how the night can inspire magical vulnerability in us that can be both spiritual and physical. The heavens and galaxies open up to us in a million wondrous ways and it's as if we become changed people. When we experience events at night, they can often feel so much more profound and intense than had we experienced them during the day. It is a time when we are more exposed and prone to discovery, a time when emotional transformations can take their deepest hold, when spirits sing to us, making us long for the unsayable. In this poem, I try to explore how that longing can manifest at night. Whether love, anguish, or both, it is the sense of being without, the muscle of a feeling that might burn inside and unroot us from ourselves.

"The School of Night," Edward Hirsch

"The School of Night" is a nocturne, a night scene, a dark vigil. In *Shakespeare and the Rival Poet* (1903), Arthur Acheson posited a secret literary and philosophical society that existed in England at the end of the sixteenth century. It supposedly took its motto from Shakespeare's *Love's Labour's Lost*: "O paradox! Black is the badge of hell, / The hue of dungeons, and the school of night." The existence of the group was never proved, but I've always liked the idea of sneaking into a gathering with Sir Walter Raleigh, Christopher Marlowe, and George Chapman, who used the idea of "night" as an esoteric and divine symbol. My poem literalizes the idea of the school of night for a speaker, an old man, a class of one, who stands on the threshold of the human and what is beyond it. That's because the nocturne is a threshold poem, a lyric of sleeplessness, the cry of the solitary and bereft.

"Expectation Nocturne," Lisa Russ Spaar

All of my poems are nocturnes, either in their subject matter or their linguistic gestures. An insomniac since childhood, I think that some conjuring of dusk and midnight deeps, of what John Ashbery called poetry's "blue rinse," always haunts my praxis. "Expectation Nocturne," a loose Shakespearean sonnet, is a night song. The poem is an apostrophic lyric of waiting, or anticipation, in the wake of the day's exigencies, hardships, and its moments of dread perhaps made more acute by the speaker's aging, her awareness of mortality ("one minute swallowing / the next, the next, the next"). The speaker addresses the night ("O sunken Well"), inverting it as Elizabeth Bishop does in her own poem "Insomnia." When the sun winks out, and the earth blackens, and the sky lights up, albeit "wild with sorrow" (like a "wary spouse" all too aware of life's "broken dishes"), the speaker nonetheless allows herself to trust its "secret blue" even when she can not fully fathom it; she has, in fact, learned to trust in unfathomability: in word, in deed, in portent.

"With Weather," Stanley Plumly

This past December, I was reminded of a time so many years ago (almost fifty)—perhaps by having a window on a lot of winter trees, mountains in the distance, and skies overcast constantly. I was living in a far-out corner of Athens County (Ohio) on a property called Woods Lake, a place I could afford. There were lots of woods, old woods, a loon-like lake, and even a cabin that was once used on the Underground Railroad. A wholly primitive yet quaint place. One of my buddies then was Mark Strand—he had, in fact, the spring before visited me at Woods Lake. Now it was a Sunday, a dark afternoon, and the phone rings. It's Mark calling from New York with a new poem—"In Celebration." A great piece. He reads it and it of course knocks me out. After his death that was the poem of his I thought of. It was cold that Sunday, I used a fireplace for heat. (On really freezing nights I slept in my clothes.) The weather, I suppose, brought it all back to me. Woods Lake was a very still and solitary place. My own "With Weather" is both an homage and an elegy. Elegies, especially, tend to be night poems. When Mark called me that late December afternoon, the day was closing down. I think the loss of light, for me, was the weather tone that got me started.

"Rock Star," Calvin Forbes

"Rock Star" has its origins many years ago when I was living in Kingston, Jamaica. My son, who was around seven years old back then, used that expression to describe someone on the TV show we were watching. Though it was not the first time I had heard this usage, I remember thinking it odd and jotted it down in my notebook. Over the years I have written various renditions of "Rock Star" with the title as a unifying metaphor or theme. I never throw any draft away and sometimes when I go back with fresh eyes something clicks and I find the right language, form, imagery, and angle into the nascent poem and it works. And sometimes it doesn't come together, but that's how it goes. And I keep trying. Patience. There's no telling how many hours or even years go into writing a poem, no matter its length. My son, who is now over forty years of age, and a father himself, doesn't remember this story. But I do.

ECLOGUES

"Eclogue," Dan Beachy-Quick

One of the poems in persistent echo in my head is Robert Duncan's "Often I am Permitted to Return to a Meadow." That meadow that, in the poem, is both mine and not mine, is both made of mind and is mind itself, feels not only a place of pure paradox in which what is impossible takes root and so becomes the possible, but also seems to me to be some ur-place of poetry's own source: meadow where the creatures graze, where song tends and cares for the creatures' well-being. Imagining that meadow has somehow become key to my sense of what Poetry is, and in the past years I've paused long enough through the relentless days to read through the pastoral tradition in Greek poetry, to read Virgil's

Eclogues, and to begin to sense how those bucolic fields even now hold themselves open, some ongoing relic of pure possibility in which peace hints at being more than a rumor. At the simplest level, my "Eclogue" seeks that meadow, asks after where it might be found—which is to say, it's a poem asking permission to return. I can guess that meadow exists at some infinite distance floating as if in space; I can guess it exists so deeply within the mind or heart it is as if at an infinite distance within us. Sometimes I think those opposites are no different at all, and the meadow is where extremes loosen their contradiction and in the deep grass make their truce.

"Forage," Sophie Cabot Black

The eclogue is a form that holds interesting possibilities—neither ruled by meter nor system, and originally being pastoral, or bucolic, the poem can easily become an argument for a life lived above the human fray. Historically, the speaker of these lines is a shepherd, or even two, in conversation, conveyed as one speaker to another, in what has been called a "miniature drama." These days it's hard to think of writing such a poem: most of us no longer work alone in nature, let alone herd sheep. But there is the argument that the 21st Century is precisely the time when one needs the pastoral, to speak about the dark through the light and from some higher ground. Initially, I wanted this poem to be between two poets as sheep herders; however, the two soon turned into the one, arguing for the enterprise of the poet/shepherd, for the backdrop of living the lonely yet Muse-d life, amongst animals other than human, the dailiness inherent in taking care.

"3 Skies," Joanna Klink

These poems, short and pastoral, draw loosely on the tradition of the eclogue. The setting of the poems is rural—set apart from the urban world—and to some degree the subject is rural life: not freedom from the complexity of "civilized" social and political ways of being, but the intensity of natural landscapes when they become the sole focus of one's attention. Although the poems aren't dramatized as dialogues in the way that classical eclogues are, there is a pattern of address: a voice is speaking to a person looking out at the night sky.

I began writing these poems after studying James Turrell's Roden Crater, an extinct volcano in the Painted Desert of northern Arizona which the artist is transforming into an observatory for the perception of time. It is not yet open to the public. I was imagining what it would be like to stand on the bowl of the volcano crater at night and feel connected to that much vastness. I wrote one poem for every night of a month, the lunar cycle. The whole sequence, *Night Sky,* began as scenes of deep night and nightfall, but eventually came to include visions, recalled at night, from the burning daylit hours.

"River Channeling in the Ear," Carey Salerno

This poem's genesis was realized in a time of grief. A young uncle had just passed away, and I felt completely drenched by his sudden passing and my brother's visible absence from the funeral and mourning proceedings. My brother was ostracized from the paternal side of my family—"devout" in their Christianity—for converting to Islam some twenty years ago. Summoning the word "family" among those who turned their backs to my brother and who continue to deny his very existence is a painful exercise. Adding to this pain is the constant pressure to keep the existence of my brother a secret from my two youngest sisters. When I'm in the middle of the secret, at ground zero in the family home, the weight is suffocating, and my brother's absence increasingly conspicuous. This poem tries to trap the lie, secret, and forced silence in a choral round, the sound work reinforcing the impenetrability of silence (in particular, white silence) and its hold over the speaker, who continues to dead-end into the anaphoric vocal carriage of the lines. The river, here, is the embodiment of the life of the lie, the life of a secret, and the deep, abiding silence it forces one to carry within it. How it deepens and widens over time.

"Eclogue in Orange & White," Elena Karina Byrne

If I had swerved from Virgil in my pastoral, it was only because of the persistence of grief found in beauty when in Nature, my place where the closest thing to a god that might be found. The poem was inspired by Werner Herzog's book *Of Walking in Ice,* a diary of his three-week pilgrimage walk from Munich to Paris to "save" his dying friend, fellow filmmaker Lotte Eisner. Taking in and adopting some of the experience, I remade the moments recalling details of my father and mother who had already passed. The italicized lines belong to Herzog and engendered a fresh consciousness for those stanzas.

"Lines at Tongdosa Temple," Christopher Merrill

"Lines at Tongdosa Temple" had a curious genesis: Brother Anthony of Taizé, the foremost living translator of Korean poetry, invited me some years ago to arrive a few days before a poetry festival in Korea so that we could stay at one of the Three Jewels Temples of Buddhism. On our last day at Tongdosa, he arranged a visit to the studio of the retired abbot, a gifted poet and calligrapher who commissioned me to write a poem commemorating the event. As Brother Anthony and I drank tea with monks, and wandered along foot paths, and gazed at the hauntingly beautiful landscape, lines of blank verse gathered in my imagination, which seemed to fall into triplets, each depicting a different aspect of spiritual life in this pastoral setting. It occurred to me that an eclogue uniting Eastern and Western poetic forms and insights might allow me to describe a particular moment of my walk in the sun—which the abbot memorialized in his own calligraphic fashion, composing a short poem of praise for the sacred time we spent together, thanks to Brother Anthony.

"Earthly Love," Nathaniel Perry

This poem is the opening section of a fifteen-part poem, all written in the same form (the rhyming Italian quatrains of trimeter we see here) and in the voice of a father speaking to a just barely born child. In that sense, I suppose, the poem takes the idea of an eclogue—a shepherd talking to another shepherd—and remakes it as the poem of a parent, who is, himself, another kind of shepherd. The eclogue, in as much as it is a form with demands, also demands a pastoral setting, and the reader can see here the woodpecker lording over that setting— the natural world that won't quite let the human speaker in. The poem, as a whole and in this excerpt, explores much the same territory as the traditional shepherd song, spooling out verses from a poet full of questions (about God, about nature, about children, about animals) who receives little in the way of answers.

"Yellow Time," Maurice Manning

I'm certain the word "eclogue" was not in my mind when I was thinking of "Yellow Time." This poem is pretty much a transcription of my thoughts and observations when I found myself walking around and around a field up the hill from our house during the latter days of summer. If there's poetry in this, it's merely my long-standing reliance on the tetrameter line, or what I usually refer to as a four-beat rhythm. This is a field I've partly mowed and partly left to Nature. And perhaps that is something of the "eclogue" tradition this poem understands—what to tend and manage, and what to leave up to Nature. My inclination is it's always up to Nature, whatever our human intentions may be. This poem, for me, is a reminder of the wisdom we don't intend, but a wisdom that simply comes to us. And then we are invited to live with it.

APHORISMS

"Intelligent Design," Jeff Martin

It is hard to live in this current world without thinking about religion, par- ticularly fundamentalism and extremism. I've always been fascinated with the concept of the eternal reward, the pearly gates, long lost loved ones, 72 virgins. If one believes that paradise and infinite happiness wait beyond the threshold of death, why value the relatively meaningless years that precede it? Perhaps to this segment of the population, the time between birth and death is merely a chrysalis of some kind, a passage. Not being a person of faith, I worry that this paradox leaves great damage in its wake. This poem attempts to take on that idea, distill it down to its most basic conundrum. The form and style drawn inspiration from The Book of Proverbs in the Hebrew Bible and the Christian Old Testament. The idea is to ask an unanswerable question.

"Aphorisms," Jake Young

I took a graduate poetry workshop where our professor asked us to share and discuss our favorite aphorisms, and encouraged us to write our own as well. We were assigned *Geary's Guide to the World's Greatest Aphorist*, a wonderful collection edited by James Geary. In his introduction, Geary outlines what he considers requirements of the aphoristic form: aphorisms are brief, personal, definitive, philosophical, and include a twist; to this Geary outlines eight primary types or subgenres of aphorisms: chiasmuses, definitions, jokes, metaphors, morals, observations, paradoxes, and pensées. Though most aphorisms fall into more than one of these categories, just as many do not adhere to all of the formal requirements that Geary notes, his explication is a good place to start when developing one's own definition of the form. What draws me to the aphorism is its heightened rhetorical awareness—their brevity intensifies our sensitivity to their syntactical construction. Because aphorisms are able to capture entire philosophies within a single utterance, the best aphorisms seem to speak beyond their own boundaries. While aphorisms are often dialectically constructed, they exist dialogically, and as such they reveal to us how the meaning in our own lives may be absolute and yet contradictory.

"The Handbook of Risk," Sophie Cabot Black

Much like poetry, an aphorism is a small place to put a lot of weight. We hear these terse wisdoms throughout our lives from those who imagine themselves filled with experience: "to err is human, to forgive divine". Or from Yoda: "Do, or do not; there is no try". Or from your grandmother: "if the shoe fits, wear it". The taut phrases that make up "The Handbook of Risk" came out of a notebook I carried around the world of high finance. As I overheard (and sometimes misheard) the expressions of those that believe they can manage risk, I found myself putting them together as if a puzzle to finish that might lead to some knowable end. Advice, admonition, prescription: I wanted these keys to the kingdom to link as they had come, as almost-couplets, open on either end so that they would spill into each next aphorism, moving as if in sequence. Yet each stanza was also to live on its own two "legs", even as the poem held together as a whole. Half collage, half playbook, I wanted these lines to act as if a true map for those who presume that financial risk can actually be managed, while at the same time addressing the more human ideas of risk: in love, in faith, in metaphysics.

"Island Music," David Baker

This small poem and its smaller sections are what remains of a longer poem—originally around forty lines, arranged in decasyllabics—about the island of St. John in the Virgin Islands. Since I wrote the poem, in May of 2017, the island has been devastated by Hurricane Maria, has suffered from the malignant neglect of the Trump administration, and has begun a partial, slow recovery. In aftersight, I see the poem anticipated some of this ebb-and-flow of things, some beautiful, inevitable patience and eerie afterlife. When I started to dig into the original draft, I was looking for bones instead of blubber, for a sheer architecture of a place and feeling, so I cut away whole sentences, whole stanzas, entire explanatory transitions. I see it is a poem about erosion; what remains are remnants, images rather than stories, feelings rather than experiences. What remains is the sound of aphorism. I love aphoristic poetry—Emily Dickinson, Antonio Porchia, Yihia Labibidi. Even amid long prose I relish the shocking clarity of aphorism in Emerson's essays or Franklin's letters. Sometimes aphorism pushes toward wisdom—the memorable nugget—but I prefer those that incline toward the unparaphrasable image, the blunt detail: the remnant, shining.

"After the End," Emma Bolden

I confess: I've never been, and probably never will be, entirely sure of what an aphorism is. I know what the dictionary says: it's a "short, pithy" statement that presents a truth. Benjamin Franklin used the term for his terse observations and advice. For Franklin, aphorisms are whittled-down weaponry, statements of exhortation meant to needle the reader into diligence, prudence, and industrious work. The language of my Alabama childhood, however, differed: from "cain't never could" to "a one-legged cat in a litter box," the aphorisms I grew up with were looser than Franklin's, more concerned with sharing a cabalistic code than a prudent piece of advice. At college in New York, I tried to strip the Southernisms from my speech, afraid people would hear the hick in my voice. Perhaps this is the reason why, when I moved back to the South, I also moved into a serious case of writer's block. I started penning two-to-four line poems, little bursts that seemed complete in brief but, at the same time, open-ended, coded, loose. I realized that I'd found my way home, literally and figuratively—and, as my grandmother might say, I was as happy as if I had good sense.

"Last Poem," Chris Green

If I were to sit down to write an aphorism, my arms and legs would splay and my head hit the desk! For me, anything aphoristic must be accidental, generally a gem mined from a longer, abandoned poem. In this case, what I've titled "Last Poem" was the last couplet of a long, winding bestiary. On their own, these two lines seem to contain the wisdom of all poems ever written. Aphorisms are not modest.

"Drinking Together," Chris Green

I was reading Joy Harjo's poem, "Perhaps the World Ends Here." Her title opened something inside of me. I began considering the sad history of alcoholism in my family... and gradually, my subjective truth gave birth to a maxim about bars and a broad sense of loss. The poem is a stanza, a small room where I am also sitting and drinking.

"Pax Americana," Karl Kirchwey

Much of my work arises from the premise that our modern experience overlays and resonates with that of earlier civilizations. Although this sonnet was composed before the election of Donald Trump as President of the United States in November of 2016, what was on my mind was recent American adventuring intended, not to fulfill the responsibilities of a superpower, but to maintain an illusory American global hegemony, and the risks that have attended upon this. The poem's title echoes the "Roman peace" achieved by constant warfare and conquest under the Emperor Augustus, and its content is borrowed from an incident related in one of the caustic *Satires* of the Roman poet Juvenal. Trump's isolationism would seem to be at odds with such a global "American peace," and yet his impulsiveness and narcissism seem the perfect counterpart to the hubris of Milo, understood here as international meddling that results in unforeseen consequences. The aphoristic tradition in poetry consists not only of wise sayings, but of offering object lessons for those who can understand them. Poetry does not merely decorate or entertain; it also teaches.

PROSE POEMS

"One could say the train is resting," Mary Jo Bang

Emily Dickinson has an eight-line poem that begins, "This is my letter to the world,/That never wrote to me,—/The simple News that Nature told,/With tender majesty." That poem, with its enigmatic em dash (Em is a nickname for Emily, *me* is a mirror-image *em*), is open to multiple interpretations. I wanted this poem to be similarly open but to gesture to the idea of the 'swan song'—an ancient poetic metaphor for a final harmonious musical utterance that comes just before the end. The 17th century Dutch engraver Reinier van Persijn illustrated a book of songs titled *Den singende swaen* (*The Singing Swan*) by Willem de Swaen. To playfully highlight the word slippage between Swaen and 'swan,' the title page of Swaen's book has an etching of a swan playing a harp, effectively making Swaen's songs 'swan songs.' When I wrote this prose poem, the 2017 Northern California Wildfires were burning out of control. If one counts the title, the poem has 14 lines, creating behind the prose arrangement a nearly-hidden echo of a sonnet, an earlier poetic form that predates the prose poem. The word sonnet comes from the Italian *sonetto*, which means 'little song' (from Latin *sonus*, sound).

"The Salvation of America," Michael Collier

When writing a prose poem, I completely lose sense of the line as an organizing principle, which is invigoratingly disorienting. I must rely more on following prose rhythms and nascent meter. I also must work against the force of linear narrative, which wants to rise up like the ghost of all prose to assert itself. "The Salvation of America" is actually a re-engineered draft of a poem that had long stymied me. Setting it in prose allowed me to discover, and then formally exploit, structural aspects of the poem that were hidden or diluted when it was part of a larger, stanzaic pattern. This was liberating and freeing as if I'd helped a prisoner escape from the jailhouse of a failed poem. Baudelaire, Rimbaud, Kafka, Borges, Bly, and James Wright have influenced how I think about the prose poem in general or, I should say, they represent my own sense of it as a surprising and useful form. Finally, prose poems, unlike a sonnet or ballad quatrain, can be found tucked away in the work of almost any great prose writer.

"Like a Polaroid / Faded," Erika T. Wurth

I've always been enamored of prose poems. Although people use that term loosely to indicate their resemblance to the look of prose, in my opinion it's shaped more specifically than that. There are narrative prose poems that work in one large block but seem to still tell a story. And I do a bit of that—but I'm more interested in how a block form in poetry can engage imagery in a different way than traditional prose and traditional poetry does.

This particular poem illustrates my burgeoning interest in the hybrid form. It's in between poetry and the nonfiction essay form. I was interested—and I often am—in the sound that the poem is creating with the slash marks in the block form. Conceptually, it illustrates how it feels to have a miscarriage later in life and be unable to conceive again. What it is like to see other people with children knowing that you may never be able to have one.

"My body does not belong to me," Gary Young

The genesis of this poem was quite simple. Encased within an MRI machine, I closed my eyes to calm myself, and while the machine made its infernal racket, I drifted back to a time spent in the Hokyoji Zen Monastery in Japan. Sitting zazen there, my mind would often drift, and seemed to be carried on the screams of cicadas that spun like a vivified wind through the woods. The two memories merged into the experience rendered in the poem. I believe the jump between one geographic location and another, between one time and another, is easier to accept or countenance when rendered in prose. The prose poem is well equipped to encourage the reader to follow such leaps. Prose is the language of newspapers, contracts, and histories; we want to believe it. If this poem were broken into lines, its trajectory would feel too obvious, too scripted or premeditated, at least for me.

"Jefferson, Midnight," Sandra Beasley

Being a memoirist and essayist complicates my ownership of the prose poem form. When a draft begins with personal experience or researched fact, I wonder: does this want to be nonfiction? The contemporary vanguard's work is sometimes barely discernible from "flash" or, if presented in sequence, the lyric essay. But a poem has no stipulated truth-value and that, for me, is its pleasure and power.

"Jefferson, Midnight" draws from writing about the Jefferson Memorial for the *Washington Post Magazine*. For several nights, I recorded what I saw. The subsequent article was at the mercy of house editorial decisions: lede, nut graf, style of pacing and syntax.

Here I'm free to splice and juxtapose, slaloming from era to era in the space of a dozen sentences. I score the language's music. I take a real phenomenon— spiders losing their grip—and change their trajectory to fall on the speaker. Three nights of observations become one distilled moment. Prose poems offer certain cues of nonfiction. But their "fiction"-ing, their palpable heightening and compression, is what claims my heart.

"Smoke When You Can't See What's on Fire," Cynthia Marie Hoffman

This poem arises from that part of the mind that always expects the worst and is capable of weaving elaborate tales from nothing. And it is about the fear of transferring these irrational fears onto one's child. I am drawn to the prose poem for the way it invites the poet to make wide-open leaps from idea to idea, granting a sort of expansive conceptual freedom, while at the same time formally enforcing a tight juxtaposition of imagery and ideas. It packs wild ramblings in a crushing box without breath, without line breaks or stanza breaks. This poetic form seems to best mirror the workings of the obsessive-compulsive mind, wherein irrational fear bangs about without rest. In poetry, we can write things we wouldn't normally say. And although it is a small space on the page, it can nonetheless be, at times, remarkably cathartic. Liberating.

"Stop Me If I've Told You This," Kimiko Hahn

I've written prose poems using an intuitive sense of this hybrid creature. When asked about a definition, I admit I squirm a bit then glance at a poetics dictionary. *What is it?* or *Why is it?* The trigger for this piece was the title and personal anecdotes collected from time spent with my father. Because his dementia caused forgetfulness, he'd repeat himself over months, and even over minutes. Here, those repetitions presented a formal possibility, a binding motif. The repetition also offered a build up of expectation and then a swerve to deviate incrementally or completely. I look for this possibility in revising poems. And here, as in a story, I felt the progression offered the portrait of a relationship that grew and changed. There is a pivot as in a poem that I could just as well think of as a story's conventional climax: "it isn't funny." In the closure, I return to "spanking": the progression is a "spiral" and not a circle because something has changed in the speaker's sense of self, the father-daughter relationship, and even for a third person, her husband. Justifying the margins visually helps me insist on the prose dimension of the genre.

"Pathetic Fallacy," Laura Kasischke

I'd been talking about the "pathetic fallacy" in an introduction to poetry class—although I'm not entirely certain that then, or now, I'm using the literary term correctly. However, as I was struggling to explain my (loose) idea about it, and how it was at work in a poem we were reading, I started to give examples: "So, like, the sad poet goes outside and the birds are weeping in the trees, but the happy poet goes out and the birds are singing in the trees—but really the birds are just, just, just . . ." Well, what *are* they doing? (I know there's an explanation for this, but since I'm not teaching ornithology, I didn't look that up.) I wasn't getting a lot of nods-of-understanding, so I went on. "You know how there's always only a traffic jam when you're running late? That's 'false feeling . . .' So, when that's in poetry . . ." Again, I wasn't being clear, because I myself wasn't all that clear. Eventually I asked someone to get out an iPhone and read us the definition. However, in the meantime, I had a long time to think about all the pathetic fallacies I've known, which were anything but fallacies: how, truly, it poured rain on the day of my first (doomed) wedding. But, of course, it was a gorgeous day in May, full of flowers and sunshine, as my father and I rode in the back of the black limo behind my mother's hearse, which was also way too poetic, too predictable, the contrasts making everything much worse. (I could go on and on, which is why I wrote the poem.) So, thinking of this in class, I eventually had to go back and say, "No—look, the depressed poet goes outside, and the birds are laughing hysterically in the trees . . ."

At first I wrote this poem with line breaks; however, because I wanted to end it with this "song" that came to me, I went back and and made it a prose poem, hoping that the little ditty at the end would be less expected, and also that it would be read as a strange diversion/surprise instead of a corny ending. I don't know if that worked, but it was behind the prose poem choice.

MIRROR POEMS

"echolalia one," Quraysh Ali Lansana

"echolalia one," is a form of verbal imitation, or when a person repeats noises, words or phrases they hear. The word itself is a sonic and linguistic delight. Though the condition is frustrating for both sender and receiver, it is much more vexing for the person who struggles with effectively communicating their thoughts and feelings. Everyone wants and needs to be understood. Echolalia is a common characteristic in people with autism spectrum disorder (ASD). I believe folks with ASD, such as my son Ari, are superheroes.

"What Happens When We Die," Oliver Baez Bendorf

This poem started with the line, "Cardinal, who died and brought you here?" which I said aloud when a cardinal landed outside my window while I was in bed. It's not fair of me to project my grief onto the cardinal, but maybe it's the ever-present possibility of someone I love visiting me in a form other than the last one I knew. The morning my grandfather died, every member of my immediate family, in Iowa, Wisconsin, Colorado, was woken up around the same time. None of us knew yet, but we all felt it. At my aunt and uncle's house, something rattled off the wall. I never could place what it was for me—some untraceable thud. As a trans poet, I'm expanded by relation to what happens when energy changes form—what holds when physicality shifts. How much can change and still be recognized? It's the same as for the first and second part of this poem, why I played the poem backward to itself once I reached the spine.

"An Action," Kimberly Grey

When I wrote this piece I was thinking of the philosopher Ludwig Wittgenstein and his thoughts on the difficulty of expression. He said, "Perhaps what is inexpressible (what I find mysterious and am not able to express) is the background against which whatever I could express has its meaning." The mirror form, the way it echoes a new thought that is at once separate but also an underlying limb of the poem, allows for different dimensions of expression to collide to create a layered thinking. I wanted to capture the feeling of being rejected by a mother, a push against our idealized vision that all mothers are unconditionally loving beings. This form allows for two different expressions of pain: one a narrative reckoning (an internalization), the other a desire to hurt back those who hurt us (an externalization). The form itself is a statement on the power of language to convey, and thus, become its own action against pain.

"Thread a Pin Through Every Door, Drop the Line," Suzannah Spaar

I wrote this poem for a friend I missed dearly, but it morphed into a project about my own relationship with space and what distance does to a space you long for (a space both interior and exterior). All longing is incomplete and transforms through the distance of travel. The distance doesn't even need to be large—even looking into a mirror is a translation of yourself. This poem is a stitching together of the self and its translation through space, time, and "the other." Borrowing language from Gaston Bachelard's *The Poetics of Space* and imagery from cooking and stitchery (traditionally associated with women's craft), the poem deploys specular and incremental repetition to bring the speaker closer to her central question: "Then onto what / toward what // do doors open? / Do they open for the world of men or // for the world of solitude?"

"Come, Slumberless," Traci Brimhall

"Come, Slumberless" was written in the early days of my parenting, when I was sleepless and afraid and hungry and deeply in love with the small human I'd made. I wrote a lot of lullabies at the time and tried to embrace the nonsense nature of the lullaby, which is often both quite soothing and occasionally ominous. For awhile I tried to use the same images across several poems to see how they would transform through form. In this near-sonnet that almost mirrors itself, I thought of the quote from 1 Corinthians about how God sees us "through a glass darkly." Mirrors used to be still dark water or made from obsidian. The reflection was obscured through darkness, but there was still a faithfulness to the original. When I tried to mirror the near-sonnet through a glass darkly, the connections between images were different—sometimes reversals, sometimes nearly lost, always surprising. I saw my unoriginal sins reflected back imperfectly, like all gods must see their makings.

"Bloom," January Gill O'Neil

I had been teaching mirror poems to my class but realized I had not written one, and loneness was the subject matter that found me. I had been reading Natasha Trethewey and Sylvia Plath—quite a range. After a few attempts, I decided to rework the heart of a poem from an otherwise dead draft. Once you find the core of meaning, the rest is wordplay. Can a poem work forwards and backwards? That is the challenge.

"The Birch Swamp," Helen Spica

This poem's form was really an accident, unplanned, but ultimately grew, by necessity, from the matter of the poem itself. When writing about this particular landscape—a flooded birch forest I visited in Northern Michigan—the physical experience of place seemed as important to the poem as any literal description I could give. The swamp creates, after all, a mirror in the true sense, as the still water about the tree trunks reflects the forest back up onto itself with astonishing clarity. To move through this space was to move through two parallel and (nearly) indistinguishable plains at once, a small horizon broken with each step. The mirror poem, where each line has its own reflection, is a formal representation of this landscape, and I see the reading of such a poem very much like the experience of walking through such a place; the concrete world pressed against its mirrored self, which, though identical in image, is fundamentally changed, and ripples away the moment one tries to know it.

"Seventy," Marilyn Nelson

Up to now I'd been ignorant of the fact that there is a name for mirroring rhymes, though of course it stands to reason that a term would exist to describe the delightfully multiplex rhymes I have noticed mostly in ghazals, by Agha Shahid Ali, Marilyn Hacker, and Heather McHugh. I must admit that this poem has no ambition to be set against those larger and more serious works: it is merely a little jeu d'esprit of rhyming; a poem written for the sheer fun of it.

"Studio with Blackened Windows," Alexandra Teague

"Studio with Blackened Windows" was inspired by an SF MOMA exhibit about the intersections of Matisse's and Diebenkorn's work—particularly the ways both artists worked to extend space through doors and windows, and a curator's note that when Diebenkorn moved to Illinois, he found the landscape so uninspiring and antithetical to painting that he ended up blacking out his studio windows.

In this poem, which draws on Diebenkorn's landscapes and figures, I wanted to use the end words' mirroring/reversing as a way to explore limits and extensions. How can inside and out extend across seeming divisions? What does it mean to see so carefully that you can't stand to see what's in front of you? What, in our current political and social moment, does it mean to imagine "the heart of this country" (where I have lived, as I have in Diebenkorn's beloved California)? The form became a way—like the mirror behind the sleeping woman's head in one painting—of extending my exploration of these questions outward and back at the same time.

"The Last Gardener of Aleppo," Valerie Wallace

I wrote "The Last Gardener of Aleppo" after watching the short video "Inside Aleppo: the tale of the flower-seller" on YouTube. The video is about Abu Wad, who with his young son Ibrahim, maintained Aleppo's last gardening center for five years during which his rebel-held area of the city was bombed by Syrian and Russian forces. The italicized lines in the poem are Abu Wad's. It was important to me to preserve his voice in the poem. After trying out various forms, a friend I shared it with noted that in a section I'd had as the last, many of the couplets seemed close to those found in ghazals. I revised the poem into couplet stanzas, and ultimately settled into a mirror form, which I hope for the reader lends the poem a sense of repeating history, complicity, and haunted-ness that I felt after watching the video.

CONCRETE POEMS

"Before Our Eyes," Eleanor Wilner

"Before Our Eyes" began in a *renshi*, a poem chain with friends Rose Auslander and Kim Hamilton, whose one rule is that the poem's title be taken from the last line of the preceding poem. Kim's last line was "nature dying before our eyes," giving me both title and initiating subject, so the shape with its length-ening lines came from the incremental proliferation of all that dying. By the time I got to the poor sloth, I was having a great time, the avalanche of loss had become comical, and the final line had clearly reached a dead end. When the imagination hits a cul-de-sac, it makes a hair-pin turn toward possibility; the reversal of meaning dictated the reversal of line length as the poem in its reflec-tion sailed toward dawn.

"Hong Kong Crane," Phillip Cozzi

At the suggestion of my graduate project advisor, I decided to attempt writing a concrete poem mixing up visual and linguistic elements. In another poetry class, we Skyped the poet H. W. Leung from his home in Hong Kong regarding his text, "The Goddess of Democracy." I was touched by the sincerity of the author and the quality of his work. I initially had planned to write a poem in the shape of a femur but then decided to write a poem in the shape of the crane. The first writing was by hand, directly into the shape of the beak-tipped bird. Modest re-writing was required when keyboarding so that the line breaks made sense and the word "balance" stood poised in the correct position.

"Obit," Victoria Chang

This poem is part of a larger series of poems called *OBIT*. These poems all look visually like this one—prose blocks meant to resemble real obituaries—the idea was that when someone you care about dies, everything else dies too. This idea appeared when I was listening to NPR about a documentary about obituaries called *Obit*, directed by Vanessa Gould. I loved how the word "obit" sounded and listening to that piece on NPR provided me with inspiration to reinvent the obituary through poems. I proceeded to write about 75 of these obits in a two-week period in a frenzy and I've been working on these for a few years now.

The constraints of the thin narrow physical obituary served as an anchor for the process of writing about grief. The form served as a frame for the poems and helped to distill grief through language and form.

"Apollinaire's Ex-Girlfriends in the Snow," Chris Green

The poem "Apollinaire's Ex-Girlfriends in the Snow" changes the weather in Apollinaire's "It's Raining." He is famous for his calligrams (calligraphy + telegram), poems that shape and thus telegraph his subject matter. In general, a concrete poem visually dramatizes its meaning, but particular to Apollinaire and to "It's Raining," he dramatizes the movement of meaningfulness through time and space. He begins his poem with "It's raining women's voices as if they had died even in memory." The poem's fives lines slant steeply as if in heavy downpour, reflecting his deep regret for the passing of life. My poem slows the falling by presenting time more as a light snow. It allows memory to linger as the words waft down the page. And in the end, it shows Apollinaire not just as the musing poet, but as an actor in his own life's forgetting and fall.

"Skyscraper," Robin Reagler

During the time when I was studying for the PhD exams in poetry, I found myself drawn to books about a field I had considered and not pursued, architecture. After reading several books about skyscrapers, I wrote this poem which addresses the hubris involved in this endeavor. I was familiar with the work of two famous women photographers who scaled the Chrysler Building and took pictures of it. That seemed like an interesting detail to include in this feminist examination of a symbolically masculine object.

"A Brief History of Writing," Ellen Rachlin and Georgiy Zhikharev

In a concrete poem, the form and content are intertwined, both supporting each other and teasing out more in a synergetic relationship. Much like that, we came together to write something that neither of us would have completed on our own. We are both attuned to the beauty of language, of writing, but writing of a certain kind—one that shows heart, and passion, and struggle for perfection, and achievement, albeit subtle, and tentative, and one that stands on the shoulders of trials and errors. Of all the history of written word, we felt the quill represented that type of writing most perfectly. And we both are somewhat confused by the paradox of new mediums which facilitate writing but tend to breed insincerity, false eloquence and linearity of thinking, which is not, in our experience, how a thought manifests itself. As we worked on this poem, there were words, and phrases, and visual ideas that we rejected, but they undoubtedly contributed to the final product. Through their crossed-out absence they forged our unity on what remained.

"A Is for Arbor," Ravi Shankar

This concrete poem is the first poem in a series that includes the letters A, B, and C. These three poems refer to different aspects of domesticity, the first three letters of the alphabet being a kind of shorthand for any basic guide, in this case for contemporary interpersonal relations. The simplicity of that notion, however, is complicated by the content of the poems themselves, which tease out the ways in which being in relation is exquisitely difficult, indeed the most difficult thing we might be called to do in a human life. Because the emotion of that calling is so pronounced, I felt the need for the strictures of an extremely confining form to help scaffold that anxious energy.

Concrete poems tend to be over-determined, because the visual shape of the poem is often so physically present in its composition, but in this case, my idea is that there is something in the actual character of that letter 'A,' how it begins in unison and then branches outwards as it proceeds towards its base, that actually takes the shape of a materializing domestic argument. From the point of concordance, a small divergence grows in time, and that's what is being described in this poem, the quiet space of the arbor surely reclaimed by the portent and violence of a Chinese new year celebration jangling any sense of interior calm. That's what some marriages can be like and the contrasting form of a basic grammar primer seemed useful to release some of that energy.

COLLAGE POEMS

"Checkpoint," David Baker

There it was, Emily Dickinson's wonderful poem about the birds in her yard, in autumn migration. In her handwriting, on her paper: the manuscript framed and hanging on the wall of the Morgan Library in New York City. It was winter of 2017, and the exhibition was titled "I'm Nobody? Who are You?: The Life and Poetry of Emily Dickinson." I don't write quickly, not usually, but I was powerfully struck by the clarity and humanness of her slender handwriting, the grayish paper, the nearness of her. I simply took her first two lines for my first line, eight syllables, verbatim. I let each phrase echo then, like a bird calling among birds, and I followed the sounds as her yard turned into my yard, as migration turned to migration, from birds to people. I wanted the sound of invitation and interrogation at the same time, of answer and resistance, or, as she writes, of "fraud" and "plausibility." Soon another set of echoes entered, including pieces of phrases I drew from a *Buzzfeed* post written to help undocumented immigrants prepare for questioning by ICE and Homeland Security. So many of us, talking and struggling and singing at once. So many on the move.

"Things I Am Beginning to Forget," Kimiko Hahn

I've learned a great deal about hybrid texts from Classical Japanese literature, hence the attribution to Sei Shonagon. She herself wrote dozens of list-like pieces about "things." In my own, I've incorporated a range of diction (email or Dickinson's poetry), tone (on the difficultly of retrieving a memory or an answer on a gynecological form), points of view (internal thought), etc. so that the effect is that of a collage. I love when, in such a mix, the juxtapositions create a kind of electricity. That is my aim. That is part of what I hope is moving.

"Wolf Cento," Simone Muench

The cento is an ancient collage form in which material is gleaned from other poetic works: an assembly of pre-existing lines that are tailored into new texts. As I've said elsewhere, centos have immense potential to engage the lyric-I in a contemporary and emotionally impactful manner because, paradoxically, through the reconfiguration of phrases by other poets, the speaker is able to assert a new voice, a new lyric-I. In other words, the cento is less ventriloquism and more discovery. Composing centos, I'm able to unearth another voice in myself that I didn't know existed, given permission to say things that I haven't yet been able, or willing, to express in a previously established voice. The act of composing centos is also archival and citational—cataloging, preserving, and resurrecting preceding material. In addition, through the cento's constraints, its recombinant nature of recycling and rearrangement, I am able to pay homage to my influences. Ultimately, I hope the cento continues to honor and expand collaborative writing while showcasing itself as a significant form of collage in contemporary poetry.

Unlike my other "wolf centos," this poem was sutured together entirely from lines and fragments by Larry Levis, and was written for a former student and editor, who became a friend. A voice that, unfortunately, has been silenced.

"The Cloistered Life of Nuns," Major Jackson

On "The Cloistered Life of Nuns": So much of my work of recent years has sought to honor the mind at work which I like to refer to as "Major's Cubist Thinking." Collaging images and thoughts as they arise during the composition process has afforded me a greater lyricism, and yet, the central notion here is "compose," which is far more complex than merely recording impressions. As many literary critics have pointed out, collage technique imitates more how the mind processes the world around it; so few of us, if any, innately order their thinking in a linear fashion as they go throughout their day. When I collage, I go about an instinctive procedure of selecting and ordering, as well as finding the syntax and transitional phrases that yields the most surprising yoking of objects. What I seek to achieve is a kind of frisson that arises from two distinct images or ideas being brought together such that they refract and illuminate a new way of seeing and understanding. Such juxtapositions in "The Cloistered Life of Nuns" gives the poem both its velocity and speed of perception as the poem circles around this notion of naturalized violence within the context of religious and metaphysical questions; I'm the type of poet who is more likely to privilege and frame questions in my poems more so than answers. If biblical texts and philosophical treatises teach us to "love" each other and all things divine, then how do we reconcile and explain the savagery and ferocity that underlines civilization, "the Ideal Republic"?

"Lesson III: The Divisions, Illustrated," Elizabeth Bradfield

The sculptor Janice Redman is my neighbor, and once a week we meet at her house for "studio days." Her studio is full of objects in the process of transformation and tools that might transform them: thread, bandsaw, rasps, stacks of colanders. We work side by side, silently influencing each other. This erasure came from a collaboration that never happened.

Janice had a pile of maps, and we thought we might make something for a local fundraiser. Both of us poked through, and on the back of one map I found text that captured me. "Lesson III" emerged. Janice and I tried to make something of it together, but in the end it was all poem. Visually, the poem's layout echoes the spaces between salvaged words and punctuation.

In the past, I'd never felt good about erasures as a poetic practice—the results had always felt more like exercises than true poems. This time, however, the erasure revealed an aspect of my own voice I hadn't yet discovered. I can only call it alchemy. Once I'd finished the poem, I was bereft. Janice didn't know where the pages had come from, where to find more. But after a few weeks of disconsolate frustration, I located the entire book online. A conversation about the nature of America is lifting out of the pages. I am not sure how long it will be sustainable or where it will lead me.

"We Listen We Pray," Martha Collins

On the first Sunday of Advent, the period leading up to Christmas, the minister of my church preached a sermon based on Longfellow's "I Heard the Bells on Christmas Day"—a poem grounded in grief. He then asked us to compose, in any form, our own "crisis literature" during the weeks that followed. At home, church bulletin in hand, I reread the morning scripture, looked over our long list of prayer requests, and settled on the practice that led to "We Listen We Pray."

With three weeks of Advent remaining, I decided to create one line per day, using only fragments of the weekly Scripture and the prayer list. The order would be mine, but the words would all come from the sources: the poem would be pure collage. By the second day, I had decided to alternate Scripture fragments with prayer request fragments, and became quite excited by juxta-positions the method allowed me. The "scripture" lines, in italics, are from the books of Mark, Isaiah, and John; the "prayer" lines reflect the progressive essence of Old Cambridge Baptist Church, which is committed to the work of social justice. My thanks to the church, and to the Rev. Cody J. Sanders, for giving me this poem.

"Found Poem: The Couple Who Lived at the Mall," Elizabeth Spires

A few years ago, I came upon a weird, wonderful article by Lisa Selin Davis about an artist couple who, as a "performance piece," lived at the mall for four years in a secret apartment. Davis's article touched on consumerism, escap-ism, and corporate hypocrisy. It also made me think about the out-of-time and out-of-touch feeling that windowless malls create, and the sad demotion of nature into no more than an irrelevant memory. The article evoked such a strong response in me—of fascination, amusement, and horror—that a found poem resulted.

Found poems see the poetry in everyday subjects and objects that, at first glance, don't seem to be "poetic": the text of a billboard, a set of instructions, a recipe in a cookbook. By cutting, excerpting, and rearranging—which is what the collage technique is all about—I tried to distill the essence of Davis's article into a poem. Maybe it's similar, though on a much smaller scale, to the way filmmakers see the cinematic possibilities in a novel?

"Hog Kaput," Kevin Prufer

My "collage" poems are almost always generated by competing anxieties—anx-ieties that play out in the largely fictional worlds of my poetry and the "real" world of my political, social, and personal beliefs. "Hog Kaput" began with a news story about the epidemic of wild hogs here in Texas—a serious problem for farmers and conservationists. But the more I read about this, the more the vocabulary of eliminating wild hogs resembled (to my ears) the vocabulary of the American right wing's discussion of the "immigrant problem" in America. That "coincidence" of vocabularies was the catalyst for the poem, creating in my mind the various speakers, stories, and perspectives at work in the poem, as well as the various fictional narratives. The trick, for me, is figuring out how to organize these various elements into a cohesive composition—a collage that makes sense both as story and as political meditation.

Biographical Notes on the Authors

Quraysh Ali Lansana is the author of many books of poetry, and the editor of many literary anthologies, including, with Kevin Coval and Nate Marshall, *The Breakbeat Poets: New American Poetry in the Age of Hip Hop*. He teaches at Holland Hall School and the Center for Poets & Writers at OSU-Tulsa.

Jordi Alonso is the author of *Honeyvoiced*, a full-length collection, and *The Lovers' Phrasebook*, a chapbook.

Cynthia Atkins is the author of *Psyche's Weathers* and *In the Event of Full Disclosure* as well as the forthcoming collection, *Still-Life With God*.

David Baker is author or editor of eighteen books, including *Swift: New and Selected Poems, Scavenger Loop: Poems*, and *Never-Ending Birds*, which was awarded the Theodore Roethke Memorial Poetry Prize. He teaches at Denison University and is Poetry Editor of *The Kenyon Review*.

Christopher Bakken is the author of three books of poetry, most recently *Eternity & Oranges*. He is the Director of Writing Workshops in Greece: Thessaloniki & Thasos. He teaches at Allegheny College.

Mary Jo Bang is the author of eight books of poems—among them, *A Doll for Throwing, Louise in Love*, and *Elegy*, which won the National Book Critics Circle Award—and a translation of Dante's *Inferno*, illustrated by Henrik Drescher. She is a Professor of English at Washington University in St. Louis.

Aliki Barnstone has published fifteen books and three chapbooks. Her most recent full-length volumes of poetry are *Dwelling* and *Bright Body*. She translated *The Collected Poems of C.P. Cavafy: A New Translation*. She currently serves as poet laureate of Missouri and is Professor of English at the University of Missouri.

Judith Baumel is the author of *The Weight of Numbers, Now*, and *The Kangaroo Girl*. She is Professor of English at Adelphi University.

Dan Beachy-Quick is a poet and essayist, author most recently of a collection of essays, fragment, and poems, *Of Silence and Song*. He teaches in the MFA

Program at Colorado State University, and his work has been supported by the Lannan and Guggenheim Foundations.

Sandra Beasley is the author of four books, most recently the poetry collection *Count the Waves*, and the editor of *Vinegar and Char: Verse from the Southern Foodways Alliance*. She lives in Washington, D.C., and teaches with the University of Tampa low-residency MFA program.

Oliver Baez Bendorf is the author of two collections of poetry, *Advantages of Being Evergreen* and *The Spectral Wilderness*. He teaches at Kalamazoo College in Michigan.

Sebastian Bitticks publishes creative writing and journalism in newspapers and magazines in Asia and the United States.

Sophie Cabot Black has three poetry collections: *The Misunderstanding Nature*, winner of the Norma Farber First Book Award, *The Descent*, winner of the Connecticut Book Award, and *The Exchange*.

Emma Bolden is the author of three books of poetry, including *House Is An Enigma* and *Maleficae*. She is Associate Editor-in-Chief of *Tupelo Quarterly*.

Elizabeth Bradfield is the author of four poetry collections, most recently *Once Removed* and *Toward Antarctica*. Her awards include a Stegner Fellowship and the Audre Lorde Prize. Founder and Editor-in-Chief of Broadsided Press, she lives on Cape Cod and works both as a naturalist at large and a professor of creative writing at Brandeis University.

Traci Brimhall is the author of three collections of poetry, most recently *Saudade* and *Our Lady of the Ruins*. She is Assistant Professor of Creative Writing at Kansas State University.

Molly McCully Brown is an essayist and poet, the author of *The Virginia State Colony for Epileptics and Feebleminded*.

Elena Karina Byrne is the author of three books, including *Squander* and *Masque*. She is the Poetry Consultant and Moderator for the *Los Angeles Times* Festival of Books and Literary Programs Director for The Ruskin Art Club.

Tina Chang, Brooklyn Poet Laureate, is the author of the poetry collections *Hybrida, Half- Lit Houses,* and *Of Gods & Strangers*. She is the co-editor of the poetry anthology *Language for a New Century: Contemporary Poetry from the Middle East, Asia, and Beyond.*

Victoria Chang is the author of four books of poems, among them *Barbie Chang* and *The Boss*, which won the PEN Center USA Literary Award and a California Book Award. She teaches at Antioch University's M.F.A. program in Los Angeles.

Michael Collier is the author of seven volumes of poetry, most recently *My Bishop and Other Poems*; a collection of essays, *Make Us Wave Back*; and a translation of *Medea*. He is Professor of English at the University of Maryland, where he is also the director of the Creative Writing Program.

Billy Collins' latest collection is *The Rain in Portugal*. He was recently made a member of the American Academy of Arts and Letters.

Martha Collins is the author of nine books of poetry, the most recent of which are *Night Unto Night* and *Admit One: An American Scrapbook*. She has also co-translated four books of Vietnamese poetry and edited three anthologies. She founded the Creative Writing Program at the University of Massachusetts-Boston and served for ten years as Pauline Delaney Professor of Creative Writing at Oberlin College.

Phillip Cozzi is an MFA student at the School of the Art Institute of Chicago. He is a Pulmonary and Critical Care physician and Chairman of Internal Medicine at Elmhurst Memorial Hospital. He has published poetry in many medical journals.

Kwame Dawes is the author of twenty-one books of poetry and numerous other books of fiction, criticism, and essays, most recently *City of Bones: A Testament*. He is Glenna Luschei Editor of *Prairie Schooner* and is Chancellor Professor of English at the University of Nebraska. Dawes is a Chancellor of the Academy of American Poets.

Oliver de la Paz is the author of four collections of poetry, among them *Post Subject: A Fable* and *The Boy in the Labyrinth*, and co-editor of *A Face to Meet the Faces: An Anthology of Contemporary Persona Poetry*. He serves as the co-chair of the Kundiman advisory board and teaches at the College of the Holy Cross.

Cornelius Eady, a poet, playwright, and songwriter, is the author of several poetry collections including *Victims of the Latest Dance Craze*, winner of the 1985 Lamont Prize, and *Brutal Imagination*. He is co-founder of the Cave Canem Foundation and is Professor of English at SUNY Stony Brook Southampton.

Martín Espada has published numerous collections of poetry, including *Vivas to Those Who Have Failed*, *The Trouble Ball*, *The Republic of Poetry*, and *Alabanza* (2003). He has received the Ruth Lilly Prize, the Shelley Memorial Award, and a Guggenheim Fellowship. His book of essays, *Zapata's Disciple*, was banned in Tucson as part of the Mexican-American Studies Program outlawed in Arizona.

Calvin Forbes teaches jazz history, literature and writing at the School of the Art of the Art Institute of Chicago. He is the author of two books of poems, *Blue Monday* and *The Shine*.

Todd Fuller is the author of two books, *60 Feet Six Inches and Other Distances from Home: the (Baseball) Life of Mose YellowHorse* and *To the Disappearance*. From 2004–2011, he served as founding president of Pawnee Nation College. Since 2011, he has worked in research development at the University of Oklahoma. He co-directs the Mark Allen Everett Poetry Series.

Forrest Gander is the author and translator of many books, including *Be With* and *Core Samples from the World*, a finalist for the Pulitzer Prize and the National Book Critics Circle Award.

Rigoberto González is the author of numerous books of poetry and prose. He is a contributing editor of *Poets & Writers* and on the board of trustees of the Association of Writers and Writing Programs (AWP). He writes a monthly column for NBC-Latino and is currently a professor at Rutgers-Newark.

Chris Green is the author of three books of poems, most recently *Résumé,* and has edited four anthologies, including *I Remember: Chicago Veterans of War*. He teaches in the English Department at DePaul University.

Kimberly Grey is the author of *The Opposite of Light: Poems*.

Kimiko Hahn's most recent collection is *Brain Fever*. Her honors include a Guggenheim Fellowship, PEN/Voelcker Award, Shelley Memorial Prize. She is a distinguished professor in the MFA Program in Creative Writing and Literary Translation at Queens College, City University of New York.

Joy Harjo, of the Mvskoke Nation, has published eight books of poetry. *Conflict Resolution for Holy Beings,* her most recent collection, was named the American Library Association's Notable Book of the Year. Her awards include the Ruth Lilly Prize from the Poetry Foundation and the Wallace Stevens Award from the Academy of American Poets.

Edward Hirsch is the author of nine books of poetry, including *Wild Gratitude,* winner of the National Book Critics Circle Award, and *Gabriel,* as well as five books of prose. He is the president of the John Simon Guggenheim Memorial Foundation.

Cynthia Marie Hoffman is the author of three poetry collections, most recently *Call Me When You Want to Talk about the Tombstones.*

Joan Houlihan is the author of five poetry collections, most recently *Shadow-feast.* She is Professor of Practice at Clark University and also teaches in the Lesley University Low-Residency MFA Program. She is founder and director of the Colrain Poetry Manuscript Conference.

Angela Jackson is the author of three chapbooks and four books of poetry, among these *And All These Roads Be Luminous: Poems Selected and New* and *It Seems like a Mighty Long Time.* She has authored two novels and five plays.

Major Jackson is the author of four collections of poetry, including *Roll Deep,* which won the 2016 Vermont Book Award. He is the Richard A. Dennis Green & Gold Professor at the University of Vermont. He serves as the Poetry Editor of *The Harvard Review.*

Kimberly Johnson is the author of three collections of poetry, most recently *Uncommon Prayer,* and of book-length translations of both Virgil and Hesiod.

Allison Joseph is the author of six full-length collections of poems, and eight chapbooks, including *Confessions of a Barefaced Woman* and *Corporal Muse.* She teaches creative writing in Carbondale, Illinois, where she is on the faculty of Southern Illinois University.

Laura Kasischke has published ten collections of poetry, most recently *Where Now: New & Selected Poems* and *The Infinitesimals.* She has been the recipient of the National Book Critics Circle Award and the Rilke Award for poetry. She teaches at the University of Michigan.

Karl Kirchwey is the author of seven books, including *Stumbling Blocks: Roman Poems* and *The Engrafted Word*. He is Professor of English and Creative Writing and Associate Dean of Faculty for the Humanities at Boston University.

Joanna Klink is the author of four books of poetry, most recently *Raptus* and *Excerpts from a Secret Prophecy*. She is the recipient of awards from the Rona Jaffe Foundation, Jeannette Haien Ballard, the American Academy of Arts and Letters, and the Trust of Amy Lowell. She teaches in the Creative Writing Program at the University of Montana.

Joy Ladin is the author of nine books of poetry, including *The Future is Trying to Tell Us Something: New and Selected Poems*. She holds the David and Ruth Gottesman Chair in English at Stern College of Yeshiva University.

Anna Leahy is the author or co-author of six books, including her poetry books *Aperture* and *Constituents*, and two books about cancer. She directs the MFA program at Chapman University.

Elizabeth Macklin is the author of two books of poetry, *A Woman Kneeling in the Big City* and *You've Just Been Told*; and the translator, from the Basque, of Kirmen Uribe's *Meanwhile Take My Hand: Poems* and other works.

Randall Mann is the author of four books of poems, most recently *Proprietary* and *Straight Razor*.

Maurice Manning is the author of six books of poetry, including *Lawrence Booth's Book of Visions* and *The Common Man*. He is on faculty in the MFA program at Warren Wilson College and the Sewanee Writing Conference, and is a professor of English at Transylvania University.

Jeff Martin is an author, editor, and the founder of Magic City Books in Tulsa, Oklahoma.

Donna Masini is the author of three books of poems, most recently *4:30 Movie*, and the novel, *About Yvonne*. She is Professor of English/Creative Writing at Hunter College.

Erika Meitner is the author of five books of poems, including *Holy Moly Carry Me* and *Ideal Cities*. She is currently an associate professor of English at Virginia Tech, where she directs the MFA and undergraduate creative writing programs.

Christopher Merrill is the author of many books of poetry and prose, including *Watch Fire*, for which he received the Lavan Younger Poets Award from the Academy of American Poets. His recent books include *Boat* (poetry), *Necessities* (prose poetry), and *Self-Portrait with Dogwood*. He directs the International Writing Program at the University of Iowa.

Jeanetta Calhoun Mish is a scholar, poet, essayist, and the 2017–18 Oklahoma State Poet Laureate. Her publications include two-full length poetry collections, *What I Learned at the War* and *Work Is Love Made Visible*; a chapbook; and a collection of essays, *Oklahomeland*. She directs the Red Earth Creative Writing M.F.A. at Oklahoma City University.

Simone Muench is the author of six full-length books, including *Orange Crush* and *Wolf Centos*. Her recent book, *Suture*, is a collection of sonnets written with Dean Rader, with whom she edited *They Said: A Multi-Genre Anthology of Contemporary Collaborative Writing*. She is Professor of English at Lewis University where she teaches creative writing and film studies.

Paul Muldoon was born in County Armagh, Northern Ireland and now lives in New York. A former radio and television producer for the BBC in Belfast, he has taught at Princeton University for thirty years. He is the author of twelve collections of poetry including *Moy Sand* and *Gravel*, for which he won the 2003 Pulitzer Prize. His most recent book is *Selected Poems 1968–2014*.

Marilyn Nelson is the author or translator of more than twenty books of poetry and prose for adults and children, including *Carver: A Life in Poems*, a Newbery Honor Book and recipient of the Boston Globe-Horn Book and the Flora Stieglitz Straus awards. Her memoir, *How I Discovered Poetry,* a Coretta Scott King Honor Book, was named one of NPR's Best Books of 2014. She is the recipient of the Frost Medal and the Lenore Marshall Prize, a former poet laureate of Connecticut, and a Chancellor of the Academy of American Poets.

Susannah Nevison is the author of two collections of poetry, *Lethal Theater* and *Teratology*. She has taught at the University of Utah and Sweet Briar College.

Aimee Nezhukumatathil is the author of four books of poetry, most recently *Oceanic*. She is poetry editor of *Orion* magazine and professor of English in The University of Mississippi's MFA program.

Duane Niatum, a member of the Klallam tribe, is the author of numerous collections of poetry. The editor of *Harper's Anthology of Twentieth Century Native American Poetry*, his most recent books of poetry include *Agate Songs on the Path of Red Cedar* and *Earth Vowels*. Niatum received the 2017 Lifetime Achievement Award from Native Writers Circle of the Americas, Returning the Gift.

John A. Nieves is the author of *Curio*. He teaches at Salisbury University in Maryland.

January Gill O'Neil is the author of *Rewilding, Misery Islands,* and *Underlife*. She is the Executive Director of the Massachusetts Poetry Festival and an Assistant Professor of English at Salem State University.

Alan Michael Parker is the author of eight books of poems, including *The Ladder*, which won the Brockman-Campbell Award, and *Long Division*, which won the North Carolina Book Award. Houchens Professor of English at Davidson College, he also teaches in the University of Tampa low-residency M.F.A. program.

Molly Peacock is the author of seven books of poems, including *The Analyst*, as well as *The Paper Garden: Mrs. Delany Begins Her Life's Work at 72*. She is the co-founder of Poetry in Motion on buses and subways and the creator of the Best Canadian Poetry series.

Nathaniel Perry is the author of *Nine Acres*. He is the editor of the *Hampden-Sydney Poetry Review* and lives in rural southside Virginia.

Stanley Plumly's most recent books are *Against Sunset* and *Elegy Landscapes: Constable and Turner and the Intimate Sublime*. Among his many awards are the *Los Angeles Times* Book Prize and the Truman Capote Award for Literary Criticism. He is Distinguished University Professor at the University of Maryland.

Kevin Prufer is the author of seven poetry collections, most recently *How He Loved Them* and *Churches*. He has also edited numerous volumes, including *New European Poets* and *New Young American Poets*. He teaches in the Creative Writing Program at the University of Houston.

Christina Pugh is the author of four books of poems including *Perception* and *Grains of the Voice*. She is a Professor in the Program for Writers at the University of Illinois at Chicago, and consulting editor for *Poetry*.

Ellen Rachlin is the author of *Permeable Divide* and *Until Crazy Catches Me*, as well as two poetry chapbooks. She serves as Treasurer of The Poetry Society of America.

Robin Reagler is the author of *Dear Red Airplane* and *Teeth & Teeth*. She is the Executive Director of Writers in the Schools (WITS) in Houston, Texas.

Martha Rhodes is the author of five poetry collections, most recently *The Thin Wall* and *The Beds*. She teaches at Sarah Lawrence College and the MFA Program for Writers at Warren Wilson College, and directs the Conference on Poetry at the Frost Place. She is the director of Four Way Books.

Carey Salerno is the executive editor and director of Alice James Books. She is the author of *Shelter* and co-editor, along with Anne Marie Macari, of *Lit From Inside: 40 Years of Poetry from Alice James Books*. She teaches creative writing for the University of Maine at Farmington.

Mary Jo Salter is the author of eight collections of poems, most recently *The Surveyors*, and a co-editor of *The Norton Anthology of Poetry*. She is Krieger-Eisenhower Professor in The Writing Seminars at Johns Hopkins University.

Elizabeth Scanlon is the editor of *The American Poetry Review*. She is the author of a book of poems, *Lonesome Gnosis,* and two chapbooks.

Grace Schulman is the author of seven books of poems, most recently *Without a Claim*. Her honors include the Frost Medal for Distinguished Lifetime Achievement in American Poetry and the Aiken Taylor Award for Modern American Poetry. She is editor of *The Poems of Marianne Moore*, and is Distinguished Professor of English, Baruch College, C.U.N.Y.

Lloyd Schwartz's most recent poetry collection is *Little Kisses*. Awarded the Pulitzer Prize in Criticism for his music reviews, he is the longtime classical-music critic for NPR's *Fresh Air*, and has edited the Library of America's *Elizabeth Bishop: Poems, Prose, & Letters* and the centennial edition of Bishop's prose. He is Frederick S. Troy Professor of English at the University of Massachusetts Boston.

Allison Seay is the author of *To See the Queen*. She is the Associate for Religion and the Arts at Saint Stephen's Episcopal Church in Richmond, Virginia.

Ravi Shankar is author, editor, or translator of thirteen books and chapbooks of poetry, including *Durable Transit: New and Selected Poetry*. He co-edited *The Golden Shovel Anthology: New Poems Honoring Gwendolyn Brooks* and is the founder of *Drunken Boat*.

Lisa Russ Spaar has published eleven books, most recently *Orexia: Poems* and *Monticello in Mind: 50 Contemporary Poems on Jefferson*. She is a professor at the University of Virginia.

Suzannah Spaar is the co-author of *Undone in Scarlet*. She is a teaching fellow at the University of Pittsburgh.

Helen Spica's poetry has appeared in literary publications including *Denver Quarterly* and *Midwestern Gothic*. She was a 2016/2017 Teaching Fellow at the School of the Art Institute of Chicago, where she taught creative writing.

Elizabeth Spires is the author of seven collections of poetry, including *Wordling*, *Now the Green Blade Rises*, *The Wave-Maker*, and *A Memory of the Future*. She has also written seven books for children, including *The Mouse of Amherst*. She is a past recipient of the Witter Bynner Prize for Poetry from the American Academy of Arts and Letters.

Ira Sukrungruang is the author of the poetry collection *In Thailand It Is Night*. He is the recipient of the 2015 American Book Award, Anita Claire Scharf Award in Poetry, and a New York Foundation for the Arts Fellowship. He is one of the founding editors of *Sweet: A Literary Confection*, and teaches in the MFA program at University of South Florida.

Tess Taylor is the author of *The Forage House* and *Work & Days*. She served as a Distinguished Fulbright US Scholar at the Seamus Heaney Centre in Queen's University in Belfast, Northern Ireland, and was most recently Anne Spencer Writer in Residence at Randolph College.

Alexandra Teague is the author of two books of poetry, most recently *The Wise and Foolish Builders*, and a novel, *The Principles Behind Flotation*, as well as co-editor of *Bullets into Bells: Poets and Citizens Respond to Gun Violence*. She is an associate professor in University of Idaho's MFA program.

Richard Tillinghast has published twelve books of poetry and five of creative nonfiction. His most recent publication is *Journeys into the Mind of the World: A Book of Places*. He has taught at Harvard University, University of California at Berkeley, the Bread Loaf Writers' Conference, and the University of Michigan.

Tony Trigilio is the author of seven volumes of poetry, including, most recently, *Inside the Walls of My Own House* and *White Noise*. He is Professor of Creative Writing at Columbia College Chicago.

Leah Umansky is the author of four books of poetry, most recently, *The Barbarous Century*. She is an English teacher in New York City and the curator of the Couplet Reading Series.

Mai Der Vang is the author of *Afterland*.

William Wadsworth is the author of one collection of poems, *The Physicist on a Cold Night Explains*. He currently teaches at Columbia University, where he is Director of Graduate and Undergraduate Creative Writing.

Valerie Wallace is the author of *House of McQueen*.

Rosanna Warren's most recent book of poems is *Ghost in a Red Hat*. She teaches in The Committee of Social Thought at the University of Chicago.

Eleanor Wilner is the author of seven books of poems, most recently *Tourist in Hell* and *The Girl with Bees in Her Hair*. She is on the graduate faculty of the MFA Program for Writers at Warren Wilson College.

Stefanie Wortman is the author of *In the Permanent Collection,* a book of poems.

Erika T. Wurth's publications include two novels, two collections of poetry, and a collection of short stories. She teaches creative writing at Western Illinois University and has been a guest writer at the Institute of American Indian Arts. She is Apache/Chickasaw/Cherokee.

David Yezzi is the author of four books of poems, including, most recently, *Birds of the Air* and *Black Sea*. He is chair of the Writing Seminars at Johns Hopkins and editor of *The Hopkins Review*.

Gary Young is the author of a dozen books of poetry and translation, including *Even So: New and Selected Poems*; *No Other Life*, which won the William Carlos Williams Award; and most recently, *That's What I Thought*. The first poet laureate of Santa Cruz County, he teaches creative writing and directs the Cowell Press at the University of California, Santa Cruz.

Jake Young is the author of *American Oak* and poetry editor for the *Chicago Quarterly Review*.

Andrew Zawacki is the author of four poetry books, including *Videotape* and *Petals of Zero Petals of One*. He has translated francophone poets Sébastian Smirou, Anne Portugal, Abdellatif Laâbi, and Philippe Soupault, as well as Slovenian writer Aleš Debeljak. He coedited the international journal *Verse* from 1996 to 2018.

Georgiy Zhikharev writes poems in Russian and occasionally in English. His full length collection is *Игра в Слова* (*Word Play*). He is the translator into Russian of *Love Begins in Winter* by Simon Van Booy. He is currently employed by J. P. Morgan Private Bank and teaches finance at Fordham University.

INDEX

ACKNOWLEDGMENTS

I would like to express immense gratitude to my editor, Gabriel Fried, for creating this anthology with me. We both extend a special acknowledgement to David Baker who offered invaluable advice along the way.

Thanks, also, to Nathanael Jones, my former student, who helped bring these pages together; to Rita Lascaro, for her painstaking work on the book's interior design; and, for proofreading, the Persea interns at the University of Missouri and, especially, Jonah Fried.

Finally, I am grateful to all the contributing poets for their outstanding work—and, in some instances, for allowing us to cajole their poems into the making specifically for *The Eloquent Poem*. The copyright to the poems remain with the author as follows:

Quraysh Ali Lansana: "descendent" and "echolalia one" © 2019 by Quraysh Ali Lansana. Reprinted by permission of the author.

Jordi Alonso: "How To:" © 2019 by Jordi Alonso. Reprinted by permission of the author.

Cynthia Atkins: "Dear Art" © 2019 by Cynthia Atkins. Reprinted by permission of the author.

David Baker: "At Dawn," "Checkpoint," and "Island Music" © 2019 by David Baker. Reprinted by permission of the author.

Christopher Bakken: "Assos" © 2019 by Christopher Bakken. Reprinted by permission of the author.

Mary Jo Bang: "One could say the train is resting" © 2019 by Mary Jo Bang. Reprinted by permission of the author.

Aliki Barnstone: "Waiting for Greece's Fate on Serifos" © 2019 by Aliki Barnstone. Reprinted by permission of the author.

Judith Baumel: "Ballad of the Bronx Zoo's Beloved" and "Hic Adelfia Clarissima Femina" © 2019 by Judith Baumel. Reprinted by permission of the author.

Dan Beachy-Quick: "Eclogue" © 2019 by Dan Beachy-Quick. Reprinted by permission of the author.

Sandra Beasley: "Jefferson, Midnight" © 2019 by Sandra Beasley. Reprinted by permission of the author.

Oliver Baez Bendorf: "What Happens When We Die" © 2019 by Oliver Baez Bendorf. Reprinted by permission of the author.

Sebastian Bitticks: "From My Lord's Estate, I Pass High Mountains, Winding Streams, Rocky Torrents, Thick Forests, and Tall Bamboo" © 2019 by Sebastian Bitticks. Reprinted by permission of the author.

Emma Bolden: "After the End" and "Departures" © 2019 by Emma Bolden. Reprinted by permission of the author.

Elizabeth Bradfield: "Lesson III: The Divisions, Illustrated" © 2019 by Elizabeth Bradfield. Reprinted by permission of the author.

Traci Brimhall: "Come, Slumberless" © 2019 by Traci Brimhall. Reprinted by permission of the author.

Sophie Cabot Black: "Forage" and "The Handbook of Risk" © 2019 by Sophie Cabot Black. Reprinted by permission of the author.

Karl Kirchwey: "Allowing That" and "Pax Americana" © 2019 by Karl Kirchwey. Reprinted by permission of the author.

Joanna Klink: "3 Skies" © 2019 by Joanna Klink. Reprinted by permission of the author.

Joy Ladin: "Political Poem" © 2019 by Joy Ladin. Reprinted by permission of the author.

Anna Leahy: "From the Word Go" © 2019 by Anna Leahy. Reprinted by permission of the author.

Elizabeth Macklin: "This River" and "With Love from Ainezalandia" © 2019 by Elizabeth Macklin. Reprinted by permission of the author.

Randall Mann: "The Summer before the Student Murders" © 2019 by Randall Mann. Reprinted by permission of the author.

Maurice Manning: "Canebreak Love and Water" and "Yellow Time" © 2019 by Maurice Manning. Reprinted by permission of the author.

Jeff Martin: "Intelligent Design" © 2019 by Jeff Martin. Reprinted by permission of the author.

Donna Masini: "Postcard: Morning Window, Venice" © 2019 by Donna Masini. Reprinted by permission of the author.

Ericka Meitner: "Letter to Hillary on the Radical Hospitality of the Body" © 2019 by Ericka Meitner. Reprinted by permission of the author.

Christopher Merrill: "Lines at Tongdosa Temple" © 2019 by Christopher Merrill. Reprinted by permission of the author.

Jeanette Calhoun Mish: "Reckoning" © 2019 by Jeanetta Calhoun Mish. Reprinted by permission of the author.

Simone Muench: "Wolf Cento" © 2019 by Simone Muench. Reprinted by permission of the author.

Paul Muldoon: *from* "Frolic and Detour" © 2019 by Paul Muldoon. Reprinted by permission of the author.

Marilyn Nelson: "Pity Eyed" and "Seventy" © 2019 by Marilyn Nelson. Reprinted by permission of the author.

Aimee Nezhukmatathil: "Aubade with Wolf Spider" © 2019 by Aimee Nezhukmatathil. Reprinted by permission of the author.

Duane Niatum: "Sleeping Woman" © 2019 by Duane Niatum. Reprinted by permission of the author.

John A. Nieves: "Buckle and Wash" and "Composition" © 2019 by John A. Nieves. Reprinted by permission of the author.

Alan Michael Parker: "The Lights Turn Blue" © 2019 by Alan Michael Parker. Reprinted by permission of the author.

Molly Peacock: "Haiku" © 2019 by Molly Peacock. Reprinted by permission of the author.

Nathaniel Perry: "Earthly Love" © 2019 by Nathaniel Perry. Reprinted by permission of the author.

Stanley Plumly: "With Weather" © 2019 by Stanley Plumly. Reprinted by permission of the author.

Kevin Prufer: "Hog Kaput" and "The Damned" © 2019 by Kevin Prufer. Reprinted by permission of the author.

Christina Pugh: "Litany" and "Shirt Noise" © 2019 by Christina Pugh. Reprinted by permission of the author.

Ellen Rachlin: "A Brief History of Writing" © 2019 by Ellen Rachlin. Reprinted by permission of the author.

Robin Reagler: "Skyscraper" © 2019 by Robin Reagler. Reprinted by permission of the author.

Martha Rhodes: "Delivery" © 2019 by Martha Rhodes. Reprinted by permission of the author.

Carey Salerno: "River Channeling in the Ear" © 2019 by Carey Salerno. Reprinted by permission of the author.

Mary Jo Salter: "Vanitas" © 2019 by Mary Jo Salter. Reprinted by permission of the author.

Elizabeth Scanlon: "Aubade" © 2019 by Elizabeth Scanlon. Reprinted by permission of the author.